TRUE CRIME : NEW YORK CITY

D0885605

0 11557 03629 9

TRUE CRIME : NEW YORK CITY

The City's Most Notorious Criminal Cases

Bryan Ethier

STACKPOLE
BOOKS

Copyright © 2010 by Stackpole Books

Published by
STACKPOLE BOOKS
5067 Ritter Road
Mechanicsburg, PA 17055
www.stackpolebooks.com

Printed in the United States of America

10 9 8 7 6 5 4 3 2 1

FIRST EDITION

Cover design by Caroline Stover

Cover photos: Stack of dollars, © Elnur/Shutterstock; Human feet with toe tag, © Pertusinas/Shutterstock; Police line tape and detective, © Ilya Andriyanov/ Shutterstock.

Library of Congress Cataloging-in-Publication Data

Ethier, Bryan.
   True crime : New York City : the city's most notorious criminal cases / Bryan Ethier. — 1st ed.
      p. cm.
   Includes bibliographical references.
   ISBN-13: 978-0-8117-3629-9 (pbk.)
   ISBN-10: 0-8117-3629-6 (pbk.)
   1. Crime—New York (State)—New York—Case studies. I. Title.
HV6795.N5E84 2010
364.109747'1—dc22
                                                            2010008996

Contents

CHAPTER 1

A Brief History of
Crime in
New York City

In New York City, crime is *big*. It's big news, big to politicians who win and lose jobs because of a flux in crime; it makes for splashy, big headlines that increase newspaper sales. Crime is big to communities that bear big pride in their neighborhoods, neighbors, and security. Finally, crime is a part of New York City lore, meriting its own historical chapter beside the city's rich entertainment, culture, art, and sports.

Big Apple crime and the press have had an intimate if not symbiotic relationship since 1835, when James Gordon Bennett Sr. established the *New York Herald*. Bennett created a newspaper that was the "eyes and ears" of the city, ferreting out information and reporting on issues that people wanted to read. He saw journalists as investigators charged with reporting stories in real time, from the crime scene, and without fear or reproach. His reporters thought nothing of uncovering the failings and blind subjectivity of the city's archaic "watchman" system of law enforcement. The city of 320,000 was protected by an unwieldy and frequently ineffective force made up of a nightwatchman and a few hundred law enforcement officers.

One of the earliest headline-grabbing murders occurred in 1841. The death of twenty-one-year-old Mary Rogers underscored the power of the press. Rogers's story, like her life, is cloaked in mystery even today. Though her birth records were lost, Mary Rogers probably was born in 1820 in Old Lyme, Connecticut. When she was seventeen, her father died in a riverboat explosion; Rogers soon began working as a clerk in a tobacco shop owned by John Anderson. In what today might be considered a form of sexual harassment, or at least poor judgment, Anderson paid her "a generous wage in part because her physical attractiveness brought in many customers." And what customers she attracted! One man claimed to have spent an entire afternoon at the store "to exchange teasing glances" with her. The *Herald* even published an admirer's poem in which he referred to her "heaven-like smile and her star-like eyes."

Not surprisingly, the popular and fetching Miss Rogers garnered newspaper headlines and articles with her purported disappearance in 1838. On October 5 of that year, the *New York Sun* reported that Rogers had disappeared from her home, and her mother, Phoebe, had discovered a suicide note, believed to be from the missing young woman. Add to this evidence a coroner's analysis of the suicide note that revealed a "fixed and unalterable determination to destroy herself," and the press and its readers had the story of all stories.

There was only one problem with the story of Rogers's disappearance: it wasn't true. A day later, the *Times* and *Commercial Intelligence* called Rogers's disappearance a hoax, reporting that she had merely gone to Brooklyn to visit a friend. But when Rogers did not immediately return to work, others suggested that her tardiness was, in fact, the ruse. When Rogers did settle back into her job, some of the press suggested her "disappearance" was a con job engineered by Anderson, ostensibly to increase sales. So much for reporters and editors checking their facts.

But that was just part one of the bizarre Mary Rogers story. On July 28, 1841, police found Rogers's body floating in the Hudson River in Hoboken, New Jersey. Just three days earlier, Rogers had told her fiancé, Daniel Payne, that she was going to visit "her aunt and some family members." She never returned.

The press jumped all over the death of the "Beautiful Cigar Girl," and the local and national papers filled their columns with sensational stories and theories about the details of her death. Those details suggested that Rogers had been murdered. Some months later, with the official inquest not complete, Payne was found dead. Investigators found in his possession a rueful note and an empty bottle of poison beside his body. The death of Mary Rogers was never solved, but it did underscore the lack of precision and accuracy with which both the press and the police operated during the nineteenth century.

Realizing the inefficiency of this system of law enforcement, the state legislature approved on May 7, 1844, a proposal to create a 1,200-man police force. One year later, under the direction of Mayor William Havemeyer, the police force was reorganized and officially established as the New York City Police Department. The city was divided into three districts, each with its own courts, magistrates, and clerks. Station houses were established.

During the 1800s, police had their hands full with riots that shook the city, in particular the 1863 Draft Riots. Also known as Draft Week, the New York Draft Riots were violent uprisings born from resistance to the new military draft laws passed by Congress. Excluding the Civil War itself, the Draft Riots represented the largest civil insurrection in American history. In order to take control of the city, President Abraham Lincoln enlisted the aid of many regiments of militia and volunteer troops. The majority of the protestors were typical working-class men, who felt they were being singled out to fight while the wealthier men were spared.

At first the protests were civil; but they became heated, then violent, and ultimately "racial." Numerous blacks were murdered in the streets. The ensuing pandemonium encouraged Maj. Gen. John E. Wool to suggest the institution of martial law. He did not, however, have the men to implement such control. Instead, the military used artillery and fixed bayonets to quash the riot and suppress the mob. In the uprising, numerous buildings and homes were destroyed, including an orphanage for black children. It is believed that as many as 120 people died and another 2,000 were injured in the Draft Riots.

Seven years later, the city was rocked by the Orange Riots. These uprisings were precipitated by British Protestants who wildly celebrated the anniversary of the 1690 Battle of the Boyne, which helped to steel Protestant rule in Ireland. Their parades, through largely Irish neighborhoods, incited the riots that led to the deaths of sixty-three predominantly Irish citizens during the police action. The NYPD was again battling rioting citizens on January 13, 1874, during the quelling of a violent protest involving thousands of people at Tompkins Square Park, the site of numerous riots. Police also fought back uprisings in Harlem.

Such protests by scores of people eventually yielded to use of political, social, and physical force by smaller clans working together in not always legal trades. These gangs in time developed into Mafia "families" in the shadows of the city's underworld.

The Mafia's rise to power in New York City began in the 1820s with thug gangs such as the "Forty Thieves" and the "Roach Guards." Believed to be named after Ali Baba and the Forty Thieves of literary fame, the Forty Thieves was the first organized street gang in New York City. Composed mainly of Irish immigrants, such gangs ran unimpeded in the city's Five Points intersection, ruling with threats of garrote and extortion.

The gangs formed as a means of rebellion against their low social status. New York's Five Points—the intersection of Canal Street, the Bowery, Broadway, and Mulberry Street—bordered the slums from which many of the Forty Thieves members came. Members soon found that the best way to rise up society's ladder and out of their mosquito- and disease-infested neighborhoods was through crime.

They met at a Centre Street grocery store where they received illegal assignments and strict quotas regarding the gang's illegal activities. Each member was given an incentive to break the law, reap the benefits of such action, and move up in stature and position. With better leadership and internal discipline in the rank and file, the Forty Thieves gang could have succeeded in its goal to create its own micro-society. Instead, the lack of cohesion led to the dismantling of the Forty Thieves, and by 1850, most of its members had moved onto larger gangs or gone their own way.

Cosa Nostra, "Our Thing," was an Italian-American criminal society, an offshoot of the Sicilian Mafia. It was spawned in New York City from small impoverished ghettos, growing into city-wide secret societies and finally into international organizations.

The New York Sicilian Mafia developed in the 1910s and 1920s from the remnants of the Five Points Gang. The New York Mob focused most of its illegal activity on gambling and theft until Prohibition was introduced in 1919. From that point, both the role and the rule of the Mob expanded significantly and quickly. Powerful, organized gangs of bootleggers arose from the resistance to the government's abolition of alcohol sales. For many of these gangsters— namely Arnold Rothstein, Meyer Lansky, and Charlie "Lucky" Luciano—the sale of illegal liquor proved to be a wildly profitable business enterprise.

From the glory days of the Mafia (1920–60), and from the rubble and carnage of wars between rival Mob gangs, emerged the Five Families of New York: Colombo, Bonanno, Gambino, Genovese, and Luchese. They controlled many of the city's industries and organizations, including liquor, drugs, prostitution, transportation, unions, and often politicians and law enforcement agencies. For the most part, the dons of these Mob clans operated with impunity from the law—more often than not, they owned the lawmakers and the law-enforcers, keeping them on their family payroll in return for free business reign in their city territories.

Gambino family boss Paul Castellano was one of the first Mafia kings to attempt to legitimize his businesses. But introducing change into a world run by antiquated rules of ancient cultures was difficult, as Big Paul learned.

In the 1980s, the face of the Mafia changed once again, this time from the sobriety of Castellano to the gregarious celebrity of John Gotti. Dubbed the "Teflon Don" because charges against him never seemed to stick, Gotti craved the limelight, especially during the occasions when he was arrested and brought to trial. Many New Yorkers and members of the press adored him; Gotti was photogenic, and his flamboyant style of operating garnered big headlines and sales for the tabloids. Still, old school mobsters eschewed the way Gotti flaunted himself in public, laughing in the face of the law. The Mafia, once so secret and mysterious, had gone prime time. By the early 1990s, the FBI had collected hundreds of hours of audio and videotape on Gotti (as it had on Castellano, ironically) discussing illegal operations of his Gambino Family. In 1992, the teflon wore off of Gotti's expensive suits, and he was arrested on thirteen charges and sentenced to life in prison. Many other Mafia associates followed Gotti to prison, as local authorities began to win the war on organized crime.

Similarly, the mid-1990s saw the New York City Police Department and the city's administration, led by Mayor David Dinkins, clean up the crack cocaine industry that had run rampant in the 1980s. During the administrations of Rudolph Giuliani (1994–2001) and current mayor Michael Bloomberg, city crime—including violent offenses—dropped by nearly one-third. In 2009, New Yorkers saw a drop in crime of more than 11 percent. The 461 city murders in 2009 marked the lowest yearly total since the NYPD began keeping reliable records in 1963.

Many credit the decrease in overall crime to improved law enforcement tactics and technologies, including the increased security presence following the September 11, 2001, terrorist attacks. The decrease in crime was good news for Bloomberg, who in 2009 won a third term in office, thanks in no small part to the reduction in the city's crime rate.

CHAPTER 2
Still Mad After All These Years

In the waning minutes of January 21, 1957, four New York City Police Department detectives, accompanied by local investigators, arrived at the Waterbury, Connecticut, home of fifty-four-year-old George Metesky. Carrying with them a search warrant for the premises, they knocked loudly on the front door. The house at 17 Fourth Street was dark, quiet inside.

Suddenly, a stout, middle-aged man opened the door. He wore pajamas and an innocent smile, like a chubby kid roused from a pleasant dream. He greeted the officers respectfully. Two women, his older sisters, huddled in the shadows, peering curiously through the front door at the cops.

In this quiet neighborhood in the factory district of Waterbury, law enforcement agencies rarely, if ever, appeared at a resident's front door in the early morning hours. But for some time, neighbors had wondered about the strange bachelor who kept odd hours and lived an even stranger life with his two older sisters. So had the police. Both cops and residents would soon confirm what George Metesky did in his spare time.

Metesky glanced at the warrant and allowed the team of investigators to enter his home, still with that steady, carefree expression on his face.

"I know why you fellows are here," he said calmly. "You think I'm the Mad Bomber."

They did. They had clues, and they had samples of his handiwork and his handwriting. To confirm their suspicions, they asked Metesky for a handwriting sample. A sample of the letter *G*, to be precise, written so distinctly in the letters penned by New York City's notorious "Mad Bomber." The unflappable Metesky continued to smile pleasantly, and he wrote the letter *G* on a piece of paper.

"What does 'F.P.' stand for?" they asked, referring to the Mad Bomber's trademark moniker on his threatening letters to the city.

"F.P. stands for fair play," said the man.

But police suspected that George Metesky and fair play were mutually exclusive. For the last sixteen years, a disgruntled individual had been randomly planting homemade bombs throughout the city. The bombings had been accompanied by unique, angry, often desperate letters to the media. Many were warnings of what would occur if the world did not acknowledge his pain. For sixteen years, this crazy's demand for "fair play" had held the city hostage, paralyzed with fear. Tonight, police would release the grip this man had held on New York.

Metesky led the police to his garage workshop, proud to show off his tools of his trade, like a kid with a new chemistry set or erector set. In the workshop was a lathe, the chief tool in this madman's home laboratory. In the house, police found pipes and connectors used in makeshift explosive devices. Also discovered were inexpensive watches, flashlight batteries, brass terminal knobs, and unmatched wool socks, often used to transport the bombs. They were the tools of the trade—tools for making bombs. Tools used by George Metesky, the Mad Bomber of New York City.

Get dressed, the investigators ordered Metesky. *We're taking you to Waterbury police headquarters for questioning.* Moments later, Metesky reappeared, dressed in a double-breasted, buttoned-up suit. It was as if he were going out on the town, and in a sense he was.

In the annals of New York City crime, few cases have stultified police more than that of the Mad Bomber. From 1940 to 1956, George Metesky planted at least thirty-three bombs in New York City theaters, terminals, libraries, public rest rooms, and business offices. Of those thirty-three, twenty-two exploded, injuring fifteen people. No one died from Metesky's homemade explosives and that was, he said, by design.

To understand how a simple man of Slavic descent who lived with two spinsters and commuted from Connecticut to his job with the Consolidated Edison Company in New York became a terrorist, you have to go back to 1931. A generator wiper by trade, Metesky one day was working when a boiler backfired and pummeled him with a blast of hot gases. The explosion sent Metesky flying, and noxious fumes clogged his lungs and choked his breath in his throat. Metesky was hurt badly and unable to work for twenty-six weeks. He collected sick pay during that time, but then lost his job. Eventually, Metesky developed pneumonia, which later developed into tuberculosis, and he blamed the illness on the accident at work. Metesky filed a claim for workman's compensation but was denied because he filed the claim too long after the accident. He appealed the denial and was rejected three times, the last in 1936.

Out of work, out of patience, and out of hope, Metesky by 1936 had come to despise Con Edison and its lawyers, as well as coworkers whose testimony in the compensation case did not weigh in his favor. Unable to vindicate himself against a group of specific men, Metesky sought revenge on anyone he could find.

A former U.S. Marine who had served in World War I, Metesky had been a specialist electrician at the U.S. Consulate in Shanghai,

China. His experience with and knowledge of electricity and electrical devices gave him the know-how to build small explosive devices. He planted his first explosive device on a windowsill at the New York City Con Edison power plant on November 16, 1940. The bomb was crudely made—nothing more than a short piece of brass tubing stuffed with gunpowder. The activator—the ignition—was made of sugar and flashlight batteries. He wrapped the device in a note and signed the paper "F.P."

Fortunately, someone found the device before it could detonate. Ironically, had the bomb worked, the note would have exploded with it, eliminating it as evidence. In September 1941, a similar bomb was spotted lying in the street, five blocks from the Con Edison headquarters building at 4 Irving Place. It was a dud, but contained no note. Investigators pondered both incidents but had no suspects.

George Metesky was a man of contradictions and perverted loyalties. Willing to kill random Americans without remorse, he nevertheless felt a deep respect for his homeland. So committed was he to his nation that for the duration of the United States's involvement in World War II, Metesky declined to make a single bomb. He declared his patriotism in a letter to the police:

I WILL MAKE NO MORE BOMB UNITS FOR THE DURATION OF THE WAR—MY PATRIOTIC FEELINGS HAVE MADE ME DECIDE THIS—LATER I WILL BRING THE CON EDISON TO JUSTICE—THEY WILL PAY FOR THEIR DASTARDLY DEEDS.

For eleven years, Metesky wreaked havoc by writing crank letters and postcards to police stations, newspapers, and, especially, Con Edison authorities. Police handwriting experts studied the block lettering on the notes and theorized from the shapes of the letters "G" and "Y" that the author was likely of European descent. They were, in hindsight, correct.

On March 29, 1951, Metesky was back at work, setting off a bomb near Grand Central Station. This was his first explosive device to detonate, and its earthshaking explosion rocked the station and passersby. No one was injured, but police investigators noted the complexity and power of this explosive compared with its predecessors. By studying the construction of the device, investigators now surmised that the bomber had a background in the military.

In rapid succession, Metesky planted bombs in a New York public library telephone booth, a phone booth at Grand Central Station, and finally at the Con Edison headquarters on Irving Place. He also mailed a bomb to the Con Edison building in White Plains. These bombs either failed to explode or did not injure anyone when they detonated. Moreover, Metesky had thus far failed to elicit the sympathy he sought from Con Edison and the community.

On October 22, 1951, the *New York Herald Tribune* received another desperate letter from Metesky:

BOMBS WILL CONTINUE UNTIL THE CONSOLIDATED EDISON COMPANY IS BROUGHT TO JUSTICE FOR THEIR DASTARDLY ACTS AGINST ME. I HAVE EXHAUSTED ALL OTHER MEANS. I INTEND WITH BOMBS TO CAUSE OTHERS TO CRY OUT FOR JUSTICE FOR ME.

In his letter, Metesky advised police to check both the Paramount Theater in Times Square and Pennsylvania Station for bombs. One was found and disabled in Times Square; none were found at the train station. On November 28, a coin-operated locker at the IRT 14th Street subway station exploded; no one was hurt. Before year's end, the *Tribune* received another letter of warning from the Mad Bomber: he would place more bombs under theater seats.

By now, the public was aware of the Mad Bomber and his intentions; so were the police. Despite the preponderance of clues, they had made only modest progress on the case. Con Edison had for months sought in its files evidence of an ex-employee injured on the job who might be carrying a vendetta. Administrators did not know that some of their old personnel files were incomplete. For the moment, George Metesky operated with impunity. Metesky planted three bombs in 1952, injuring his first individual; police responded by downplaying the incidents and asking newspapers to refrain from publishing Metesky's letters.

Meanwhile, Metesky's devices of terror were becoming more sophisticated. Over the next four years, Metesky planted numerous bombs throughout the most populated sites in the city. Only a few caused even minor injuries, but New Yorkers were more agitated than ever. No place was safe—not the movie theaters, the subway, or the trains. Even Radio City Music Hall, with its lovely, senti- mental holiday programs, was not exempt from Metesky's chi- canery. Perhaps the most bizarre incident occurred on November 7, 1954, during a performance of Bing Crosby's *White Christmas*. With an enthralled audience of 6,200 on hand, Metesky exploded a bomb, hidden in the bottom cushion of a fifteenth-row seat. The seat was so densely padded that only patrons in the immediate area heard the explosion. While the movie continued to play, police took four injured patrons to the theater's first aid room. Police moved fifty people from the immediate crime area to seats in the back section of the building. For the next ninety minutes, the huge audience enjoyed the film and the subsequent stage act, none the wiser.

Metesky's trail of terror continued. In 1956, a seventy-four-year- old men's room attendant at Pennsylvania Station was plunging a clogged toilet when a bomb exploded in the bowl. Fragments of porcelain pierced the man like a spray of bullets, and the power of the explosion nearly ended his life. Among the fragments found were a watch frame and a wool sock.

Subsequent bombings produced odd results that bordered on travesty, because of the benighted public's responses to the traps Metesky laid. One day, a guard at the RCA building at Rockefeller Center found a small length of pipe in a telephone booth. He alerted another enterprising colleague who decided the five-inch metal tube would make an interesting "plumbing project." Notwithstanding the rash of bombings in New York, this "insightful" laborer carried the pipe with him on the bus ride back to his home in New Jersey. At home, he laid the device on his kitchen table and went to bed. The next morning, he was awakened by a deafening *bang* as his "plumbing project" blew a hole in his table and his bowl of cornflakes.

Likewise, a New York Public Library clerk left his common sense in a library telephone booth. While attempting to use the phone, he dropped the coin onto the floor. When he bent over to retrieve the coin, he spotted a maroon sock attached to the shelf. The sock held an iron pipe with a threaded cap on each end. Like the guard at the RCA building, the library clerk showed an error in judgment by not contacting authorities. He consulted with his work colleagues, and then hurled the device out the window and into Bryant Park. Within minutes the bomb squad and more than sixty New York City police officers and detectives were descending upon the scene.

If one incident kicked the police investigation into overdrive, it was the December 2 bombing at the Paramount Theater in Brooklyn. At 7:55 P.M., a bomb tore through the theater, injuring six of the theater's 1,500 occupants. Fortunately, no one was killed, but everyone knew the Mad Bomber was back at work. Police commissioner Stephen P. Kennedy ordered a manhunt unlike any other. The bombing and the commissioner's announcement made for thunderous newspaper headlines. But announcements and newspaper headlines were doing little to catch the Mad Bomber.

Paranoia overwhelmed New York City. Some citizens fingered their neighbors as potential bombers, and police were inclined to interview each individual. In the pre-computer age, such investigations were time-consuming and exhausting. Investigators also laboriously searched legal records, mental hospital admissions, and vocational schools for any clue to the bomber's identity.

Con Edison continued to search its employee files for clues to the bomber's identity. But they, like the police, were deluged with hundreds of other leads, tips, and copycat letters from the general public, and each tip had to be investigated. A Bomb Investigation Unit had been created in April 1956, and the department had issued a multi-state alert for someone with mechanical skills who could operate a lathe or drill press (used in making pipe bombs). The person posted mail from the White Plains area, and "had a deep hatred of the Consolidated Edison Company." The department then circulated a picture showing a pipe bomb similar to the type Metesky built. Police similarly distributed descriptions of the bomber's letters and requested those who recognized the handwriting to report to the police department. Investigation into drivers' license applications in the White Plains area found five hundred that bore similarities to the bomber's handwriting. Now it was the NYPD's job to interview each of the five hundred individuals with handwriting similar to that on the bomber's letters to the newspapers. Finally, on December 27, 1956, the New York City Board of Estimate and the Patrolmen's Benevolent Association posted a $26,000 reward for the capture of the Mad Bomber of New York.

Ultimately, it took the work of two people, initially mere bystanders, and some luck for the police to finally identify the Mad Bomber and strap a straitjacket on George Metesky and his acts of terrorism. Inspector Howard Finney of the New York City crime lab was a pragmatic, scientific man with a master's degree in forensic criminology. He was not one to think out of the box, per se, or in this case, out of the Mad Bomber's mind. When a colleague suggested Finney ask a psychiatrist to do a criminal profile of the killer, Finney balked. But after further considering the slow progress on the case, Finney contacted respected psychiatrist Dr. James Brussel, who had had some moderate success in helping police with this experimental criminal profiling.

Brussel had his own private practice, but also served as the Assistant Commissioner of Mental Hygiene for the State of New York. Through his position, Brussel had consulted with police on numerous occasions. He did not think he had anything to offer this case, however. In his memoir *The Casebook of a Criminal Psychiatrist*,

Brussel explained that psychiatry was not always precise, especially in profiling, which was just in its infancy. Still, Brussel agreed to lend his support and input. He started by reading the case file on the Mad Bomber and quickly concluded that the person was almost "certainly mad."

What today may be considered overwhelming forensic evidence was to police in the mid-1950s very little to go on. Still, Dr. Brussel was able to draw conclusions about the identity of the bomber based on the slightest evidence. Brussel concluded that the Mad Bomber was male (most bombers historically have been men), held a grudge against Con Ed, and was likely a former employee. The psychiatrist also believed that the madman had been injured by the company and was seeking revenge. He felt that the Mad Bomber believed that the energy company and society were conspiring against him.

As Brussel saw it, the Mad Bomber was a "textbook paranoid." Brussel expanded his critique: the madman was around age fifty, was neat, "meticulous, and skilled at his work." Brussel drew these conclusions from the neat lettering of Metesky's letters to the media, the careful construction of the bombs, and the high standards of the work (such perfection was common in paranoid individuals, said Brussel). Also of note, Brussel said:

> The bomber was foreign or spent the majority of his time with foreign people. The bomber wrote in stilted, formal language bereft of any contemporary slang. He utilized phrases like "dastardly deeds" that sounded as if out of Victorian fiction. He referred to Con Edison as "the Con Edison" when New Yorkers had referred to the utility giant without the article "the" for years.
>
> The bomber had at least a high school education but probably no college. The stilted language of the letters and skilled construction of the bombs spoke of self-education. The excellent handwriting indicated at least some formal schooling.
>
> The bomber was a Slav and probably Roman Catholic. Culturally speaking, Eastern and Central Europeans most often employ bombs as weapons. Most Slavs are Catholic.

The bomber lived in Connecticut, not New York. Some of the letters had been mailed from Westchester Country (a location in between Connecticut and New York) and Connecticut was home to large communities of Eastern and Central Europeans.

The bomber suffered from an Oedipal Complex. Like most Oedipal sufferers he was likely unmarried and lived with a single female relative or relatives that were not his mother. He probably lost his mother young.

Dr. Brussel made these conclusions based on the phallic construction of the bombs; the strange (and breast-like) W's in the bomber's otherwise perfect handwriting, and the strange slashing and penetration of the movie theater's seats. As far as Finney and his detectives were concerned, these were Brussel's most farfetched conclusions, but the doctor was confident in them.

Ironically, Brussel also said that the killer would be wearing a double-breasted suit when captured by police. Brussel's profiling reinforced much of what the police already suspected about the bomber; Finney, though impressed, agreed that the description of the Mad Bomber could match that of hundreds of men. What could they do to home in on the Bomber's identity?

Brussel's advice surprised Finney. To date, the police had discouraged newspapers from printing the Made Bomber's letters, hoping he would cease his attacks once deprived of attention. Brussel advised Finney to do just the opposite: spotlight the Mad Bomber's mad letters and activities, and ferret him out like a rodent.

Finney feared that encouraging MB would pique his anger and increase the bombings. Not so, argued Brussel. The Mad Bomber was a man who thrived on attention but also desperately needed to be caught. Profile him in every newspaper possible, Brussel suggested, and let him come forward to correct any errors in the descriptions presented. On December 25, newspapers published articles on a Christmas Eve bomb found at the New York City Public Library along with a profile of the presumed bomber. The next day, the *New*

York Journal American published an article in conjunction with the police department urging the Mad Bomber to surrender, in return for a "Fair Trial." The paper also agreed to publish the Mad Bomber's "grievances" against Con Edison. Not surprisingly, the department heard from every crackpot in the city, claiming to be the Mad Bomber. By the end of December 1956, bomb hoaxes and false confessions had risen to epidemic proportions. At the peak of the hysteria, December 28, police received more than fifty false bomb alarms.

A few of the would-be Mad Bombers came close to fitting Metesky's profile. One Upper West Side resident lived with an aunt and often fiddled with metal; neighbors claimed he left at odd hours of the night and carried suspicious-looking packages. Police investigated the man and discovered that he was a sculptor who sold his works in Greenwich Village. Another dubious married fellow from Darien, Connecticut, was reported by neighbors to travel to New York frequently, always carrying a blue valise. Police interviewed the man, opened the valise, and found a pair of women's high-heeled boots. In a turbulent marriage with a woman ten years his senior, the man often met with prostitutes in the city. As police also learned, the man had a foot fetish and made the women he met wear the boots during periods of intimacy. Brussel's interest was piqued when he learned of a man with a grudge against Con Edison. Brussel examined the man's medical file and learned the man had been confined to a mental hospital on one of the days of the attacks, however.

The police and the media did, however, hear from another man glad to help them with their case—the Mad Bomber himself. Metesky responded to the newspaper article by refusing to turn himself in. He continued to promise to "bring Con. Edison to justice." Metesky signed the letter "F.P.," meaning "Fair Play." He also listed the sites of bombs he'd placed that year. Were there some explosive devices that investigators had not found?

Wrote Metesky: "My days on earth are numbered—most of my adult life has been spent in bed—my one consolation is—that I can strike back—even from my grave—for the dastardly acts against me."

Meteksy's letter was more revealing; he claimed to prefer using the more powerful pistol powder over shotgun powder in his bombs. Metesky also stated he'd been injured on the job at the Con Edison site and referred to himself as totally "disabled"; he said that he had to pay his own medical bills, and according to Metesky's letter, that "Con Edison had blocked his workers' compensation case."

The *Journal American* ran an edited version of Metesky's letter on January 15, 1957, and asked for "further details and dates" regarding the original compensation case. Perhaps it could arrange for another compensation hearing.

The Mad Bomber was doing just as Brussel expected; he was showing his hand. George Metesky was close to becoming a real person to the frightened residents of New York City.

The newspaper received Metesky's third and most revealing letter on January 19, 1957. Here, Metesky lamented how Con Edison employees allegedly ignored him when he suffered. He complained that workers failed to notice him for hours as he lay injured on the cold concrete.

After nearly seventeen years, Metesky could not release the resentment and bitterness he'd built up for his former employer. So enraged was he at Con Edison that he did the unthinkable: he contacted Dr. Brussel himself. He only identified himself as F.P. The conversation was brief, and Metesky got to the point: "Keep out of this, or you'll be sorry."

He hung up the telephone before the call could be traced. Dr. Brussel smiled. His analysis of Metesky's psyche was correct, and his ploy to lure the Mad Bomber from hiding was working.

But it took the work of one patient, detail-oriented woman to finally crack the Mad Bomber case. As she had been doing for some time, Con Edison records clerk Alice Kelly was busy sifting through piles of records on former Con Edison employees. She, like many other company employees, had been charged with matching troublesome ex-employees with the profiles rendered by police and the psychiatrist. Finding an angry worker who fit the profile was a daunting task; as its named implied, Consolidated Edison was a massive organization, built from the merger of several other smaller utility companies in the 1920s and 1930s. While records from the post-merger years were in good order and easily accessed, paperwork from the pre-merger days was a mess, lumped together by a number of divergent filing methods. Brussel believed the Mad Bomber could have been a middle-aged man who worked in one of the smaller power companies. One day, shortly before the dawn of the new year, Kelly stumbled across the file of a former employee named George Metesky, of Waterbury, Connecticut. He'd worked for United Electric and Power Company, and his description and work history matched that provided by the police. A wide-eyed Kelly read through Metesky's file: He had suffered an "on-site injury . . . and blamed his subsequent tuberculosis on that accident—a claim that could not be proven. After his disability claim was denied, Metesky had written several angry letters to the company—one promising revenge for the firm's 'dastardly deeds.'"

She brought the file to her superior . . . Could she have broken open the case and found the man who'd terrorized New Yorkers for sixteen years?

Metesky, meanwhile, continued his cat-and-mouse game with the police and Dr. Brussel. After all these years, the Mad Bomber figured his only nemesis was the police. Surely, Con Edison had nothing to connect him with the bombings. He was wrong, as he learned on the fateful January night when police arrived at his door.

With an air of delight, Metesky gladly confessed the details of his sixteen-year terror spree. In return, he was charged with attempted murder, damaging a building by explosion, maliciously endangering life, and carrying concealed weapons. All told, forty-seven charges were leveled against Metesky.

In the wake of the arrest, residents of Fourth Street were stunned when their neighbor was identified as the Mad Bomber of New York. Metesky was, for most residents of the street, an enigma. Neighbors commented that they wondered what he did for a living—if he actually worked. What did he do during his frequent trips to New York, in a $4,000 Daimler provided by his doting sisters? Most curious, what was he building in his garage at all hours of the day and night? Why did a generally polite yet distant man live alone with two older sisters, who, it would be learned later, worked in a button factory to support him? Some children even dubbed the house at number 17 the "Crazy House," even though there was never any real sign of foul play.

Others noticed, however, that this odd man began to change shortly before his arrest. At about the time newspapers began to publish the profile of the Mad Bomber, Metesky began to reach out to his neighbors. Perhaps the public profile of him was cathartic; perhaps Metesky subconsciously knew that the end was near, and his sixteen years of bitterness and self-torture were coming to an end. Whatever the reason, he began to speak to neighbors, even occasionally helping a local kid to fix a model airplane. Had they only known that a clinically paranoid man did live down the street from them, the curious neighbors might have taken substantive action against Metesky and reduced some of the emotional and physical damage he inflicted upon the city.

As it was, as January 21, 1957, became the 22nd, police had in their possession arguably the most notorious terrorist in recent history. Metesky, though bold and brazen in his public correspondences and attacks on the city, was quite ill, both physically and mentally. Tuberculosis had eaten away at his body, and bitterness had consumed his soul. And maybe that's what saved his life.

George Metesky never went to trial despite confessing to the bombings. After a team of psychiatric experts examined him, Judge Samuel S. Liebowitz declared Metesky mentally incompetent and committed him to the Matteawan State Hospital for the criminally insane. Suffering from severe tuberculosis and acute paranoia, Metesky failed to respond to psychiatric treatment, even from Dr. Brussel. His physical health did, however, improve; in time, he overcame the tuberculosis and focused his efforts on being released from the hospital. The *Journal American* hired a lawyer to appeal Metesky's rejected 1931 claim for workman's compensation "on the grounds that Metesky was mentally incompetent at the time and did not waive his rights."

The appeal was rejected. Curiously, Metesky made it clear to Dr. Brussel that he had built his explosive devices in such a way that they would not kill anyone. One time, Brussel asked Metesky if he considered himself crazy. Metesky, patient and polite as he often was, simply smiled and said no. Ultimately, authorities in the psychiatric field agreed.

In 1973 the U.S. Supreme Court ruled "that a mentally ill defendant cannot be committed to a hospital operated by the New York State Department of Correctional Services unless a jury finds him dangerous." Metesky had never had a trial by jury; consequently, he was transferred to the state hospital Creedmoor Psychiatric Center. The Center had no affiliation with the correctional system and, after determining that Metesky was harmless, it released him. On December 13, 1973, George Metesky returned to his Waterbury home and his workshop. The only stipulation to his freedom: he had to make monthly visits to a local mental health clinic.

He lived for another twenty years, peacefully and quietly, in his Waterbury home, and left the world less mad and less *mad*.

CHAPTER 3
As Neighbors Watched . . .

When Catherine Genovese left Ev's 11th Hour Sports Bar on Jamaica Avenue in Hollis, Queens, on the night of March 13, 1964, she had no indication that her obituary would become a footnote in a social-psychology textbook. The twenty-eight-year-old barkeep and cafe manager, popularly called "Kitty," climbed into her red Fiat that night and made the short drive to her home in the Kew Gardens section of the city. She pulled the car into a spot in the parking lot of the adjacent Kew Gardens Long Island Railroad, got out of the car, and locked it.

It was around 3:15 A.M. and the typically quiet neighborhood, with its tree-lined streets and shops and Tudor-style buildings, was buttoned up tightly on what was one of the coldest nights of the year. Genovese had made the short walk from the parking lot to her second-story apartment at 82–70 Austin Street hundreds of times, always cautious but never terrified. A native New Yorker, she was petite in size (barely over five feet) but tough-minded. She liked the excitement of the city and all that came with it—good and bad.

But on this night, the "bad" was about to occur.

After taking just a few steps toward her home, Genovese caught in the corner of her eye the image of a man walking toward her. She paused. She noted that he was a black man, no one she recognized. Genovese began to run. So did the man. He pulled a knife from his pocket and held it high as he streaked toward her.

Could she reach her apartment door, located behind the building? Or perhaps the local bar a few doors down the street? What about the police call box that was posted at the corner of Austin Street and Lefferts Boulevard?

Kitty Genovese had no time to turn those thoughts into action. Her assailant was too fast, too intent on killing a woman on this night. He captured her near a streetlight at the end of the parking lot and jumped onto her back. He stabbed her at least twice, feeling a hunter's rush of excitement as he did. Genovese was as shocked as she was physically wounded. She screamed, "Oh my God, he stabbed me! Help me! Please help me! Please help me!"

Under optimum conditions, many of the residents in the neighborhood could have heard Genovese's cries for help, could have witnessed the attack, and might have done something to prevent her murder. But the night's chill and the late hour had forced most families to shut their windows, muting her calls. Still, a few curious residents turned on their lights to see what was happening. What was the racket? A tussle spilled out of the nearby bar? A lovers' quarrel? Irene Frost at 82–68 Austin Street heard Genovese's cry for help. She'd later testify in court that she saw the "injured woman lying on the ground, pleading for assistance." Up on the seventh floor of the same building, Robert Mozer opened his window. "Let that girl alone!" he yelled. The assailant paused, ran off, and moved his car, away from sight. Then the neighborhood went silent and dark.

Genovese, meanwhile, was seriously injured and bleeding badly. Somehow, she mustered enough willpower and strength to drag herself to her feet and creep around the building. She was desperate for help. Would it come?

After moving his car, the assailant returned to the crime scene, wearing a wide-brimmed hat. He searched the parking lot and apartment complex and finally followed the trail of blood to a doorway at the rear of the building in which Genovese lived. He found her lying in a vestibule, semiconscious. The man took his time, cut off her bra and panties, and raped her. He concluded the assault by stealing $49 from her. As she lay, moaning and incoherent, he stabbed her, again and again. Then he left her to die.

With this second act of the heinous crime, lights again flicked on in some apartments. Some residents opened their windows and craned their heads to see what was happening on the street below. Samuel Koshkin lived with his wife on the sixth floor of 82–40 Austin Street and wanted to call the police, but his wife kept him from doing so. Surely others already had made the call, she cautioned. Another female resident who lived on the second floor also heard the attack and saw a "girl lying down on the pavement with a man bending down over her, beating her."

Shortly after the final blows were struck, at least one witness called police. But this was 1964, years before the implementation of a national 911 emergency line. Whether the police reacted immediately to the first call is unclear. When the first officers arrived at the crime scene, they discovered in a first-floor hallway the battered and bloodied body of a woman. An empty wallet lay on the floor, beside her body. Police identified the victim as Catherine Genovese. At around 4:15 A.M. rescue workers took away Genovese by ambulance. But by this point, it was too late. She died of asphyxiation en route to the hospital.

The entire assault and murder took about thirty-two minutes. But the story that followed has endured to this day, leaping from the pages of the NYPD investigative reports to the front pages of newspapers, and finally into psychology textbooks. Through her death, Kitty Genovese revealed another side of human nature.

For the twelve to twenty-four hours following Genovese's death, NYPD detectives rushed into a furious and, ostensibly, thorough investigation of the murder. They fought frigid temperatures and sharp winter winds that made the job of interviewing neighbors that much more chilling. Within hours, according to the *New York Times*, "they discovered at least 38 people who had heard or observed some part of the fatal assault on Kitty Genovese."

Thirty eight people who literally stood by, idly, and did nothing to rescue Kitty Genovese from her killer.

When police questioned the neighbors' apparent apathy during the attacks on Genovese, they received more than a few odd responses. One tenant thought "a lovers' quarrel" was occurring. Another witness admitted to being afraid of intervening. Others weren't sure what they were seeing on the street below, so they erred on the side of caution and did nothing. One witness admitted being too "tired" to respond. The list of excuses grew and baffled investigators. Had the inaction of these neighbors, and perhaps other neighbors, cost Genovese her life? Or could it be that such "witness-shy" persons were behaving quite naturally, under the circumstances?

In time, all of America would learn more about this "shy witness" syndrome. For now, however, New Yorkers, the police, and the press were busy searching for a killer. Their first order of business: discover the motive behind the killing.

Kitty Genovese was the oldest child of Vincent and Rachel Genovese. Vincent and his family grew up in Brooklyn in the 1940s and '50s and started his own coat and apron business, the Bay Ridge Coat and Apron Supply Company. Reasonably successful in business, Vincent moved his family to upscale New Canaan, Connecticut, in 1954. The move was precipitated when Rachel witnessed a shooting near their New York home. By now, Kitty was nineteen, finding her way in life, and liked the city. She decided to stay in the suburbs.

Petite, with dark hair and a pleasant if not quite pretty face, Kitty Genovese was outgoing and sociable, and she enjoyed Latin American music and dancing. A 1954 graduate of Brooklyn's Prospect Heights High School, she was bright and articulate, and could discourse on a breadth of subjects from art to history to politics.

Were she born and raised in a different era, in a different culture that provided more opportunities for working women, she might have furthered her education, perhaps pursued a career that utilized her artistic bent and understanding of life's finer qualities. Instead, she got a job as a bar manager at Ev's 11th Hour Sports Bar, a small neighborhood bar some five miles from her Queens apartment. This job allowed her to utilize her people skills, and Kitty Genovese was hard not to like. Genovese was ahead of her time in other ways as well: she was a lesbian. While same-sex relationships are now commonplace, nearly fifty years ago a lesbian relationship was considered taboo in most social circles.

Despite living in Queens, Genovese visited her family in New Canaan on most weekends. They were a close-knit family, and Genovese hoped to one day open her own Italian restaurant with her father in New Canaan. Genovese's parents worried about her living so close to the bustling-yet-edgy big city. But she was approaching thirty years of age, and she had to make her own decisions, her parents realized.

So why would anyone wish to harm Kitty Genovese? It took investigators little time to find the answer to that question.

Finding the man who had ended Genovese's life and turned the Kew Gardens neighborhood emotionally inside out was not particularly difficult for the thirty detectives who were the vanguard of the investigation. A milkman whose deliveries took him through Kew Gardens and Forest Hills provided a description of a suspect. Other witnesses added depth to the description furnished by the milkman. Yes, they had seen a man with this description in the neighborhood prior to the murder.

Police now had a serviceable description of the potential killer. And they had luck on their side. About one week after the murder, they arrested a man for stealing a television set during a home burglary. The man, ironically, fit the description of the suspect in the Kitty Genovese murder. His name was Winston Moseley.

Moseley, twenty-nine, hardly fit the bill of a stereotypical killer and burglar. He was just five-feet-eight, thin, with a dull, droopy face. He was married, had two children, owned a home in Queens, and was a professional machine operator. He had no criminal record until his arrest on March 19, 1964.

Shortly after his arrest for burglary, Moseley confessed to killing Genovese—and to the surprise of the investigators, two other individuals: Barbara Kralik, age fifteen, in July, and Annie Mae Johnson, twenty-four, in February. Both murders occurred in Queens, Moseley said.

Police, however, found his confessions incredible, at least initially. Police already had in custody eighteen-year-old local gang member Alvin "the Monster" Mitchell. Mitchell had already confessed to the murders of both Johnson and Kralik.

Moseley was adamant that he had killed both women, however. He added that he'd committed or attempted numerous sexual assaults, rapes, burglaries, and robberies of many other women. Based on these admissions, additional investigation, and an evaluation by a respected psychiatrist, police concluded that Moseley was their guy. The June 11, 1964, edition of the *New York Daily News* trumpeted the headline "Moseley Tells How He Killed 3."

The subsequent trial revealed that Moseley was a man haunted by bizarre urges that he could not control, destructive compulsions to act aggressively toward women. So the murder of Genovese, the defense said, was the act of a criminally insane man. To wit: Moseley was cool and composed in his recitation to the packed courthouse.

When referring to the murder of Johnson, Moseley said, "I intended to kill her. I didn't think she was dead, so I shot her again." He also said he raped her and then dragged her body into her home and then set it on fire. In the Kralik case, Moseley said he initially wanted to rape the girl; when he heard someone inside Kralik's house, Moseley took his knife and stabbed the girl repeatedly. A hushed courtroom listened to his chilling confessions.

Then Moseley revisited the Genovese killing. On the night of March 13, Moseley said he left his house, intent on killing someone.

"When I got such a thought it remained with me regardless of what else I might be thinking," said Moseley.

On June 11, 1964, the defense and prosecution summed up their cases before the eleven-man, one-woman jury. Defense attorney Sidney G. Sparrow urged the jury to render a "not guilty by reason of insanity" verdict. Moseley had lived a "Jekyll and Hyde" existence. By day, Moseley was a hard-working man who took care of his family; after sunset, however, he turned into a deranged killer. Surely, these were the actions of an insane man, Sparrow argued. Moreover, would a sane man begin to assault a woman, leave to move his car, then return to finish the job when "10, 20, 30 or 50 people were opening windows, opening and closing doors, yelling at him?"

Assistant District Attorney Frank Cacciatore rebuked Sparrow soundly: Moseley was a "panther, a beast, roaming the streets of Queens in the dead of night," he proclaimed to the jury. Try as Sparrow might, the jury scoffed at his argument. After deliberating for seven hours, the jury announced its decision: Moseley was guilty of murder in the first degree. The next day, the *Daily News* announced the decision: "Crowd Applauds as Queens Jury Dooms Moseley," its headline read.

Moseley was initially convicted of murder and sentenced to death. However, in 1967, the New York Court of Appeals reduced the sentence to life imprisonment. It found that after a trial court had found him legally insane, Moseley should have had the right to plead "medically insane" at the sentencing hearing. Today, he remains behind bars, denied parole at least thirteen times.

Kitty Genovese might have been just another murder victim, just another statistic in New York City's ledger of violent crimes. But two weeks after her death, the *New York Times* published an article that changed the way many people thought about New Yorkers and the death of Kitty Genovese. Suddenly, with one cover story, the Genovese murder had gone national.

The headline of the article, attributed to Martin Gansberg on March 27, 1964, was as inaccurate as it was sensational: "Thirty-Eight Who Saw Murder Didn't Call the Police."

"For more than half an hour 38 respectable, law-abiding citizens in Queens watched a killer stalk and stab a woman in three separate attacks in Kew Gardens," Gansberg wrote. "Twice their chatter and the sudden glow of their bedroom lights interrupted him and frightened him off. Each time he returned, sought her out, and stabbed her again. Not one person telephoned the police during the assault; one witness called after the woman was dead."

Gansberg's article underscored the belief that the residents of Kew Gardens did not react to the assault-turned-murder. The one man who did call for help, according to Gansberg, told police: "I didn't want to get involved." One housewife said, "We thought it was a lovers' quarrel." Another husband and wife said, "Frankly, we were afraid." Another woman said, "I didn't want my husband to get involved."

One other man said he heard the disturbance and turned on his light to get a better view of the ruckus. He did nothing to stop it. Why? "I don't know," he shrugged. Still another man refused to act "because he was tired and went back to bed."

Assistant Chief Inspector Frederick M. Lussen, head of the borough's detectives, said he was shocked by the neighbors' indifference to the murder. The "good people" failed to call the police, he said. "As we have reconstructed the crime, the assailant had three chances to kill this woman during a 35-minute period. He returned twice to complete the job. If we had been called when he first attacked, the woman might not be dead now."

Lussen's statement echoed the sentiments of the author and was an indictment of the residents of Kew Gardens. The *Times* article cast an image of the city and its people that readers across the nation would struggle to accept. Were New Yorkers really that cold and uncaring?

Subsequent investigation—by both public agencies and private individuals—has rewritten the inaccurate version of the truth reported in the *Times* and, to some extent, history.

Joseph DeMay, a lawyer, historian, and longtime resident of Kew Gardens, in 2000 constructed a Web site that provided a pictorial history of the Kew Gardens neighborhood. He also conducted a personal investigation of the crime, and his written analysis and reconstruction of the murder is one of the most popular and respected analyses on the Genovese case.

DeMay claims thirty-eight people did not witness the crime in its entirety. Only three people, it is believed, saw one of the stabbings. Unlike early reports, DeMay concurs with subsequent police investigations that Moseley attacked Genovese twice, and not three times, as initially reported. The entire assault and murder lasted thirty-two minutes, with the second attack occurring in the ground hallway of the building, out of view of all but one witness. The first attack, on Austin Street, probably came and went before neighbors had a chance to react. According to further police investigation, corroborated by DeMay's own findings, only two witnesses, Joseph Fink and Andree Picq, are known to have seen the first attack.

Similarly, the Queens district attorney concurred in his written briefs that witnesses probably got to their windows after the first attack had occurred, again validating the conclusion that thirty-eight people did not witness the murder.

Some witnesses claimed that noise from the neighborhood bar, Old Bailey, a few doors from Austin Street, may have muffled Genovese's cries for help. However, according to one local newspaper, the bar had been shut down before midnight, due to "fighting among patrons, a common occurrence that neighbors constantly complained about."

The first attack occurred near a street light, which, some experts still argue, would have created a "stage-like" scene for the assault. However, this conclusion, says DeMay, is based on the power and light range of a modern lamp. According to an affidavit filed by surviving witness and retired NYPD officer Michael Hoffman, "the original street light was not very bright." Moseley's testimony concurred. Illumination, or lack thereof, casts yet more light upon this shadowy and obfuscated case. Although Moseley reportedly moved his white Corvair to avoid identification, he also testified that he was not worried about being identified during his second attack because "it was late at night and I was pretty sure that nobody could see that well out of the window."

Also of note, unlike today when surveillance cameras and bright lights hover above parking lots and garages as mechanical watchdogs, the Kew Gardens railroad parking lot was not lit. Most of the ambient lighting would have come from the moon. Poor lighting may have also made it difficult for witnesses to determine whether Genovese was being stabbed or merely having one of the near-nightly domestic quarrels outside the bar. Add the bounty of trees that beautified the neighborhood but also obscured the street, and it's easy to see why neighbors may have neglected to respond to the attacks.

Ultimately, whether one person or a crowd of people witnessed a portion of the murder or the entire half-hour attack, the Genovese case sparked immediate and long-lasting interest in this trend of "diffused responsibility," also called the "bystander effect" and "the psychology of avoidance." In 1968, social psychologists John Darley and Bibb Latane conducted a study on why witnesses to emergencies and crimes often freeze and are unable to assist. Their research showed that the greater the number of people at the scene of a crime or emergency, the lower the probability that an individual will act. Darley and Latane postulated that large crowds of witnesses encourage individuals to downplay the severity of the incident, even if their instincts suggest otherwise. Witnesses to such moments of high tension may retreat from the situation because they feel inadequate to help. Again, the larger the audience to the event, the easier it is for the individual to disassociate. The work of Darley, Latane, and others helped to validate as a social-psychological trend the "Bystander Effect," a.k.a. "the Genovese Syndrome."

CHAPTER 4
The Devil
Made Me Do It

Rrrruffff . . . *Rurrrffff . . . Kill, David, KILL!* The man's head pounded with the intensity of Harvey's command.

Grrrowwllll . . . Obey me and kill those women!!! The man glared at the black Labrador. Its incessant barking was driving the man crazy! Crazier! He wanted to kill the dog. He didn't want to kill those women—no! NO! But he had to. And that demon dog kept telling him to do so.

Stop barking, Harvey!!!!! The man screamed inside his mind, clutching his aching head. *Stop ordering me!* he thought. But the demon dog's voice was too strong, too loud and powerful for the man to resist.

His body shaking violently, his mind obsessed with killing, the man dug up a .44-caliber Carter Arms Bulldog, a powerful five-shot revolver that could blow away a man, not to mention a canine. Possessed by rage, confusion, and countless other emotions, the man

33

left his Yonkers apartment. He jumped into a yellow compact car and drove to the Pelham Bay section of New York City.

At about this same time—shortly after 1 A.M. on July 29, 1976—Mike and Rose Lauria had just returned from a pleasant evening of dining at a favorite restaurant. Outside their apartment, their eighteen-year-old daughter Donna and her nineteen-year-old friend Jody Valenti sat in Valenti's Oldsmobile, reliving the evening's fun had at a New Rochelle disco, the Peachtree. Before her parents entered the apartment, Donna suggested to her father that they walk the family's poodle before retiring to bed. He agreed.

As this happened, Valenti prepared to leave. Donna opened the door, but was startled and annoyed to see a man walking their way. "Now what is this?" she asked, but stopped in mid-sentence.

Now within just a few feet of the car and the girl, the man pulled the revolver from a brown paper bag. He crouched, as Valenti and Donna sat in terror. He raised the gun, aimed, and fired three shots. The first entered Donna's chest, killing her almost immediately. The second slammed into Valenti's thigh. The third missed both girls. Then the shooter calmly turned and walked away.

Valenti survived the shooting, but when questioned by police said she did not recognize her assailant. She described him as "a white male in his thirties with a fair complexion, standing about five foot nine and weighing about 160 pounds. His hair was short, dark, and curly, in a 'mod style.'"

Other witnesses described seeing a man fitting that description, sitting in a yellow car parked behind Valenti's.

Police quickly formed two hypotheses: first, the shooter might have been a former lover seeking revenge against the girl; second, with the recent rash of Mafia activity in the area, the shooting may have been an assassination attempt gone badly. Mike Lauria, they noted, was a member of the local Teamsters union. Neither working theory was correct.

The man who later confessed to the shooting was neither in the Mob nor a disgruntled ex-sweetheart, though he did resent members of the opposite sex. His name was David Berkowitz, and he was on his way to becoming one of the most notorious serial killers in New York City history.

From July 29, 1976, to July 31, 1977, Berkowitz terrorized New Yorkers with a series of killings that made George Metesky's reign as the city's Mad Bomber seem like little more than a bad joke. Before his arrest in August 1977, Berkowitz killed six people and wounded seven others, according to his subsequent confession. He claimed he was commanded to do so by a neighbor's black Labrador that barked endlessly. Berkowitz later amended his confession, saying he'd killed just three and wounded four others. He attributed the other shootings to a satanic cult to which he belonged.

Berkowitz's story is rife with contradictions, falsehoods, and illusions. Some experts say his trial, confession, and the police investigation that punished Berkowitz's crimes with a 365-year prison term also held similar untruths, fabrications, and anomalies. Whatever the case, for one year, Berkowitz so terrified New Yorkers that people not only were afraid to leave their homes, but were quick to accuse others of being the killer called "The Son of Sam."

Two factors in Berkowitz's life led to his killing spree: his involvement in fanatical religious organizations, and his troubled relationships with the opposite sex.

Berkowitz was born Richard David Falco, in Brooklyn, on June 1, 1953. By his own admission, he entered the world with "a demon that has been living in me since birth." Although officially listed as the son of Betty Broder and Anthony Falco, the pair had long since separated after having one daughter. Betty Falco was having an affair with a married man named Joseph Kleinman, who was the real father of her son. Although Kleinman at first suggested Betty abort the baby, the woman declined. Kleinman refused to provide child support, and he threatened to leave her if she had the child. Because of these threats, Betty decided to give the baby up for adoption. She went to term and named the boy Richard David Falco.

A week later the baby boy was adopted by hardware store owners Nathan and Pearl Berkowitz; they switched his first and middle names and gave him their surname. They also gave their son David plenty of love and attention. For a while, at least, the Berkowitzes were David's salvation from a home that lacked basic familial support. If the Berkowitzes were guilty of anything, it was being socially awkward. Like his reserved adoptive parents, David grew up reticent, reluctant to seek crowds. Even at a young age, he pondered suicide. He often burned his toys, a precursor to his adolescent fascination with arson.

In September 2006, author Steve Fishman interviewed Berkowitz for an article for *New York* magazine. Berkowitz expressed a strong interest in the 1968 Roman Polanski film *Rosemary's Baby*, the classic story of a couple whose baby is the son of Satan. "I felt like it (the film) was speaking directly to me," Berkowitz said. "I stayed in my closet. I ran from the light into darkness, as the Bible says."

It was part of the "Devil's master plan," added Berkowitz

As a teen, he considered himself too gawky and big compared with his peers. Perhaps it was the wild, wiry hair; a puckish, boyish face that featured eyes that cut through one's soul; or his awkward pudginess. David may have shied away from people, but he was comfortable in a setting where independence was frowned upon—the baseball diamond. He was a talented ballplayer. His reticence eventually morphed into a vicious streak; why David Berkowitz eventually became a neighborhood bully is unclear. But his adoptive parents struggled to harness his hyperactivity and violent outbursts.

The death of David's adoptive mother had a huge effect on him. Pearl had beaten breast cancer before she and Nat had adopted David. In 1965, the cancer returned. She beat it once again, only to suffer a recurrence two years later. This time fourteen-year-old David Berkowitz truly recognized his mother's suffering, watching how the chemotherapy treatments ate away at her body and her soul. When Pearl Berkowitz died in the autumn of 1967, a piece of David Berkowitz's soul died with her.

"After Mother's death," Berkowitz said in the *New York* article, "I lost the capacity to love."

And he lost his grip on reality and his faith. Born Jewish, he'd become a practicing Catholic early in his life. Now, his faith in God also waned until he finally began to believe that Pearl's death was part of a divine conspiracy against him. To protect himself, David Berkowitz sunk further into himself, his thoughts, his fears, and his demons.

The next life-changing event in Berkowitz's life occurred in 1971, when his father remarried. From the outset of the relationship, Berkowitz had disliked the woman. The couple responded to the lack of familial affinity by moving to a retirement center in Florida. Alone, with little purpose in life, and even less direction, David Berkowitz grounded himself emotionally and mentally by cloistering himself in his fantasies.

But his fantasies had sparked another vice: pyromania. Lighting fires—this was an action over which Berkowitz felt he had some control, a way he could scream out "Help me!" Prior to his arrest, Berkowitz would start more than one thousand fires in New York City, chronicling each one in a diary, before turning to murder to assuage his own internal inferno.

Perhaps Berkowitz needed to see a flame lick its way up a piece of timber because there was absolutely no flame in his love life. The one romantic relationship he did enjoy existed more in his mind than in reality; the woman considered him just a friend, though he thought otherwise.

In 1971, Berkowitz shifted his focus and joined the army. During his three-year stint, he became an excellent marksman and a specialist with a rifle. During that time, he converted to the Baptist faith, then lost his interest in religion altogether. He had another disappointing relationship with a woman, a Korean prostitute. Berkowitz did not fall in love, but he did catch a venereal disease. He left the service in 1974.

In time he learned that his biological mother, Betty Falco, was alive and living in Queens. He desperately wished to start a relationship with her, and he began the attempted reconciliation by slipping a Mother's Day card in her mailbox. His mother was thrilled, and Berkowitz himself felt a glimmer of hope that he finally was forming a successful relationship with a female. He even met his half-sister, Roslyn. Mother and daughter worked hard to assimilate David into the family, but in time he drifted away from them also, unable to come to grips with his mother's decision to give him up for adoption. Roslyn was the "keeper." He was the child sacrificed to the world.

Women. The sight of them, the thought of them, being with them, was making Berkowitz's psychological demons rage uncontrollably. He expressed his despair in a letter to his father in late 1974. In the note, Berkowitz lamented the cold and gloomy New York weather, rivaling it to his gloomy mood. He said his world was "getting dark now." In his 1980 book *Son of Sam*, Lawrence Klausner quotes Berkowitz:

> Dad, the world is getting dark now. I can feel it more and more. The people, they are developing a hatred for me. You wouldn't believe how much some people hate me. I don't even know these people, but still they hate me. Most of them are young. I walk down the street and they spit and kick at me. The girls call me ugly and they bother me the most. The guys just laugh; anyhow, things will soon change for the better.

There is little indication that anyone close to David Berkowitz recognized the depth of his mental illness.

After writing to his father, Berkowitz began to write on the walls of his apartment, evocative statements that underscored the depth of his torture: "In this hole lived the Wicked King. Kill for my master. I turn children into killers."

And Berkowitz turned to the occult. Around 1975, he joined a religious cult called Process Group of the Final Judgment that included Sam, John, and Michael Carr, individuals who would soon play a key role in Berkowitz's life. Berkowitz attended meetings where he and cult members pledged their devotion to the devil or to Samhain, their Druid devil. From that entity, David Berkowitz coined the moniker "Son of Sam." At first the group committed small-time arson and animal sacrifices, dedicating the animals' lives "to our Gods." They made a pact with the devil, said Berkowitz, and they made a binding contract with each other. They became "soldiers of Satan," and David Berkowitz was their chief "button man." Berkowitz would later accuse cult members of committing or assisting in some of the murders for which he was indicted.

Eventually, the influences of the cult and the voices in his head forced David Berkowitz to act out his dark internal drama. It was the only way to quiet the demons' voices, he concluded. On Christmas Eve 1975, he left his home, wielding a hunting knife. He was on the hunt, and there was no question what his quarry was—a female. Any female would do, for killing a female would also kill his demons, he believed. Berkowitz drove around the city for hours, looking for his prey, listening internally for guidance from the demon voices.

His first victim may have existed only in David Berkowitz's imagination. He spotted a woman emerging from a grocery store. "She has to be sacrificed," the voices in his mind ordered. Berkowitz sprang at the woman, the hunting knife held high in the air. He plunged it into her back, once, then again. At first, the woman just stared at her assailant. Then, she screamed and took off. When police later investigated Berkowitz's story, they were unable to confirm this assault took place, however.

Police *were* able to confirm what happened next. That same night, Berkowitz spotted another young woman, fifteen-year-old Michelle Forman. Wielding the knife, Berkowitz sneaked up from behind her. He stabbed her in the head six times, seriously injuring her. Still, the girl fought for her life. Berkowitz, stunned that the bloodied victim would fight back, raced off, leaving her flailing and screaming for help. Forman struggled to a nearby apartment building and called for help. Berkowitz, his demons now sated, ambled off to a hamburger joint to satisfy his appetite.

Forman did recover from her injuries, and Berkowitz returned to his job as a security guard. Shortly after the attack, he moved to a two-family house in Yonkers owned by Jack and Nann Cassara.

Here, the demons came alive and the "conspiracy against David Berkowitz" intensified even more.

At his home in the Bronx, Berkowitz's demons had lived in his mind and soul. He soon found that those demons took on a physical form in his Yonkers neighborhood. Here, most neighbors were quiet and minded their business. Their dogs did not, however. The Cassaras owned a German shepherd who enjoyed barking, especially when tied up outside. When the shepherd barked, other neighborhood canines joined in the aria. Their barking drove Berkowitz wild, and soon he began to theorize that the Cassaras were a part of a demon conspiracy charged with driving him mad . . . driving him to kill. In his twisted mind, Berkowitz transformed Jack Cassara into "General Jack Cosmo, commander in chief of all the dogs that tormented him."

In her article for the TruTV Crime Library, Marilyn Bardsley quoted the killer: "When I moved in the Cassaras seemed very nice and quiet," said Berkowitz. "But they tricked me. They lied. I thought they were members of the human race. They weren't! Suddenly the Cassaras began to show up with the demons. They began to howl and cry out. 'Blood and death!' They called out the names of the masters! The Blood Monster, John Wheaties, General Jack Cosmo."

The dogs barked angrily at Berkowitz, taunting him, demanding blood to sate their appetites. Soon, their howls transformed into a language he understood: *Kill, David, Kill!!*

Berkowitz's grasp on sanity was gossamer thin. He had to shut out the demands of the dog demons. He desperately wanted peace in his life. He screamed at the mutts: "Be quiet!" He screamed at the demons in his head: "Be quiet!" The voices, the barks, the howls, the commands grew louder. Eventually, Berkowitz again packed up and moved, trying in vain to flee himself, but unable to do so.

He ended up not far away, in a small apartment on Pine Street. His neighbor, Sam Carr, owned a black Labrador named Harvey. By nature, labs are gentle, affectionate dogs that make excellent pets. They also are intuitive and often sense the true demeanor and psyche of a human. Harvey seemed to sense the confusion, paranoia, and evil in David Berkowitz. Harvey voiced his dislike of Berkowitz, vocally, loudly, and frequently. The demons had now merged into one demon dog—Harvey. Berkowitz was sure Harvey was possessed.

Kill, David, kill.

Shut up, Harvey! Leave me alone!

Kill, David, kill women! Harvey commanded.

Leave me alone, Harvey!!

Harvey grabbed for Berkowitz's soul . . . and, just maybe, thought Berkowitz, so did Sam Carr. Sam Carr was, David Berkowitz concluded, possessed by Satan himself. Sam Carr worked for General Jack Cosmo, Berkowitz decided. Berkowitz warned others: "Watch out for this man; he is dangerous." In Berkowitz's mind, this Sam could only be eliminated by God himself at Armageddon.

For all intents and purposes, this once-religious young man, awkward around the opposite sex, had gone past the point of no return. His only defense against, and release from, the demons was to kill.

After his 1976 murder of Donna Lauria, Berkowitz felt a deep—and rare—sense of accomplishment and fulfillment. He had done the job perfectly, professionally. Still, this feeling was short-lived. Three months later, Berkowitz was back at it. On October 23, 1976, twenty-year-old Carl Denaro was out partying with a group of friends, celebrating his pending enlistment in the Air Force. Among the friends was Rosemary Keenan, whom he knew from college. After the get-together disbanded, somewhere between 1:30 and 2:30 A.M., the couple drove home. They stopped near her home, parked the car, and began talking. Suddenly, a man walked up to the passenger's side window; he drew a gun and fired five shots. One shot struck Denaro in the head, wounding him. Panicking, Keenan drove the car back to the bar, where friends transported Denaro to the hospital. The bullet had shattered part of Denaro's skull, which surgeons had to replace with a metal plate. He was never the same, physically or mentally.

Police determined that the slugs found in the car were .44-caliber bullets. Still, investigators made little progress in the case; the shootings had occurred in different boroughs of New York City, investigated by different police departments. Though the attacks were similar in style, investigators did not yet have enough evidence to find a common thread.

Berkowitz's vendetta against women continued the following month. This time, the victims were sixteen-year-old Donna DeMasi and her eighteen-year-old friend Joanne Lomino. The two had just returned home from a late movie when they noticed a man following them. When he was close enough to be heard, the assailant said, "Do you know where . . ."

He did not finish his question. Instead, he drew a gun from inside his jacket and fired, hitting and injuring both girls. He then fired the rest of his rounds at a nearby house and fled. The pandemonium in the street awakened Lomino's family, who sped into the street to help the girls. They rushed the injured girls to the hospital where the staff determined DeMasi would recover from her injuries. Lomino was less fortunate; the bullet had battered her spine, rendering her a paraplegic for life.

At this stage, police had nothing to connect the crimes; they had occurred in two distant locations, Queens and the Bronx. Furthermore, investigators had recovered just one bullet intact. It took a third chilling murder for police to get their first clue of a pattern to the crimes.

On the evening of January 30, 1977, Christine Freund and her boyfriend John Diel were returning home from a night out. They walked together, clearly transfixed by each other, toward Diel's car. They were too much in love at the moment to notice a strange man watching them from afar. They got into the car, still oblivious to the approaching stranger. As they talked and cuddled, the stranger raised his gun and fired. Two shots blew through the windshield, striking Freund in the head. Stunned, she grabbed at her bleeding head; Diel took her head and rested it on the driver's seat and then he raced off for help. Diel tried to stop passing cars; but it was after midnight, and no one was about to stop for a frantic man waving, wild-eyed, at them. By now, Diel's fiancée was losing precious blood, and he was running out of hope.

While Diel was unable to flag down any drivers, people in the homes near the assault did hear the gunfire. Soon police arrived on the scene. But the damage had been done; a few hours later Freund died from the gunshot wounds she'd suffered. She was twenty-six years old.

The third murder gave police their first substantive clues into the psyche, if not the identity, of the killer. Detective Sergeant Joe Coffey and Captain Joe Borrelli were both assigned to the case. After the Freund murder, they concluded that the killer either was a psychopath or was someone with a grudge against Freund. But what did he look like? That was a question that would lead to years of controversy. Composite sketches from the Lauria-Valenti shooting portrayed the killer with wiry black hair; conversely, the police sketches from the Lomino-DeMasi attack had the shooter with blond hair. Could there be more than one assailant?

Investigators arrived at their theories from a few pieces of evidence. First, the bullets used in all three kills were unusual—they had come from a powerful, large-caliber gun. Coffey also found commonalities in all the assaults. He believed the killer was using a .44 and stalking women throughout the city. Ballistics did prove the weapon used was a .44 Charter Arms Bulldog. As he gathered more clues and evidence, Coffey proceeded with the investigation as if he were hunting down a psycho bent on stalking every woman in the city.

And he was.

The next attack broke the trend of earlier killings. This time, the killer went for a single woman. Columbia University student Virginia Voskerichian, age nineteen, lived just a short distance from where Christine Freund was shot. At around 7:30 P.M., on March 8, 1977, Voskerichian was walking home after completing her classes when she was attacked. Unlike the other victims, Voskerichian had enough warning and time to defend herself. As the assailant aimed his gun at her, Voskerichian lifted her textbooks to shield her body. Nevertheless, the shot penetrated the books, striking her in the head and killing her. The assailant ran.

Meanwhile, a local resident who had heard the shots raced to the scene. In so doing, he passed a male who was a "short, husky boy, 16 to 18 years old and clean shaven, wearing a sweater and watch cap, who was sprinting from the crime scene." The neighbor said the young man pulled the hat over his face and cried "Jesus," as he ran by. Others reported seeing a similar teenager, one who matched Berkowitz's description. The youth was "loitering separately in the area for about an hour before the shooting." From these statements, local media in the following days began to refer to the suspect as a "chubby teenager."

With his city abuzz with fear, New York City mayor Abraham Beame called a press conference on March 10, 1977, attended by NYC officials. He announced that the same .44-caliber Bulldog revolver had killed Lauria and Voskerichian. (Later, however, official documents revealed that the evidence was inconclusive.)

That same day, Operation Omega Task Force debuted publicly. This assemblage of top-flight investigators was charged with one task: catching the Son of Sam. Led by Deputy Inspector Timothy J. Dowd, the force consisted of more than two hundred of the city's top police officers, including Capt. Joe Borrelli and Sgt. Joseph Coffey.

At this stage of the investigation, police surmised that the shooter had a "vendetta against women," probably based on negative past experiences with the opposite sex. They also declared the "chubby teenager" a witness in the last murder, not a suspect. An earlier witness's depiction of a tall man with wiry black hair better fit the mold, police added.

Local television stations and newspapers fanned the sparks of fear spreading across the city. Their reports on the killings made front-page headlines and top-of-the-hour radio and television stories.

Not since George Metesky, the Mad Bomber of New York City, tormented the city with bombings in the '50s and '60s had New Yorkers been forced to be this vigilant.

On April 19, 1977, the .44 Caliber Killer struck again, just a few blocks from the Bronx site of the Lauria-Valenti shooting. This new attack came at around 3 A.M. Alexander Esau, age twenty, and Valentina Suriani, eighteen, were both killed. Suriani died at the scene, but Esau survived for several hours. He was not able to identify his assailant, however.

These murders included a new piece of evidence, a letter from the killer, left in the street near the attack. The majority of the note was written in block capital letters, sprinkled with a few lowercase letters. It had been addressed to NYPD Capt. Joseph Borrelli, and it was rife with spelling errors:

I am deeply hurt by your calling me a wemon hater! I am not. But I am a monster. I am the "Son of Sam." I am a little brat. When father Sam gets drunk he gets mean. He beats his family. Sometimes he ties me up to the back of the house. Other times he locks me in the garage. Sam loves to drink blood. "Go out and kill," commans father Sam. Behind our house some rest. Mostly young— raped and slaughtered—their blood drained—just bones now. Papa Sam keeps me locked in the attic too. I can't get out but I look out the attic window and watch the world go by. I feel like an outsider. I am on a different wavelength then everybody else—programmed too kill. However, to stop me you must kill me. Attention all police: Shoot me first—shoot to kill or else keep out of my way or you will die! Papa Sam is old now. He needs some blood to preserve his youth. He has had too many heart attacks. "Ugh, me hoot, it hurts, sonny boy." I miss my pretty princess most of all. She's resting in our ladies house. But I'll see her soon. I am the "Monster"— "Beelzebub"—the chubby behemouth. I love to hunt. Prowling the streets looking for fair game—tasty meat. The wemon of Queens are the prettyist of allo. It must be the water they drink. I live for the hunt—my life. Blood for papa. Mr. Borrelli, sir, I don't want to kill anymore. No msur, no moiré but I must, 'honor thy father.' I want to make love to the world. I love people. I don't belong on earth. Return me to yahoos. To the people of Queens, I love you. And I want to wish all of you a happy Easter. May God bless you in this life and in the next. And for now, I say goodbye and goodnight. Police: Let me haunt you with these words: I'll be back! I'll be back! To be interpreted as—bang, bang, bang, bang, bang, bang—ugh! Yours in murder, Mr. Monster.

The letter remained out of view from a public already anxious over the recent skein of killings. For the NYPD, gleaning the identity of the killer from such a bizarre, enigmatic letter was impossible. Still, police did theorize that the originator might be fluent in Scottish English, based on the phrase, "me hoot, it hurts, sonny boy,' perhaps a Scotch version of "my heart, it hurts, sonny boy." Police also opined that the shooter blamed a dark-haired nurse for his father's death; this speculation came from the phrase "too many heart attacks." Also, Lauria and Valenti both were in the medical field.

On May 26, 1977, police released a psychological profile of the suspect, based on input from several psychiatrists. He was described as "neurotic and probably suffering from paranoid schizophrenia and believed himself to be a victim of demonic possession." The profile perfectly fit David Berkowitz, still at large, still roaming the streets of New York City anonymously.

Based on evidence from the bullets and the profile, police questioned the owners of some fifty-six .44 Bulldog revolvers legally registered in the city. They forensically tested each gun, eliminating all as the murder weapon. Undercover officers also dressed as lovers, in traps designed to draw out the shooter. That tact also failed.

On May 30, 1977, *New York Daily News* columnist Jimmy Breslin received a most unusual handwritten letter. The author claimed to be the .44 Caliber Shooter. The note was postmarked earlier that same day, in Englewood, New Jersey. On the back side of the envelope was printed the following eerie words: "Blood and Family/Darkness and Death/Absolute Depravity/.44." The letter was equally unnerving.

Hello from the gutters of N.Y.C. which are filled with dog manure, vomit, stale wine, urine and blood. Hello from the sewers of N.Y.C. which swallow up these delicacies when they are washed away by the sweeper trucks. Hello from the cracks in the sidewalks of N.Y.C. and from the ants that dwell in these cracks and feed in the dried blood of the dead that has settled into the cracks. J.B., I'm just dropping you a line to let you know that I appreciate your interest in those recent and horrendous .44 killings. I also want to tell you that I read your column daily and I find it quite informative. Tell me Jim, what will you have for July twenty-ninth? You can forget about me if you like because I don't care for publicity. However you must not forget Donna Lauria and you cannot let the people forget her either. She was a very, very sweet girl but Sam's a thirsty lad and he won't let me stop killing until he gets his fill of blood. Mr. Breslin, sir, don't think that because you haven't heard from me for a while that I went to sleep. No, rather, I am still here. Like a spirit roaming the night. Thirsty, hungry, seldom stopping to rest; anxious to please Sam. I love my work. Now, the void has been filled. Perhaps we shall meet face to face someday or perhaps I will be blown away by cops with smoking .38's. Whatever, if I shall be fortunate enough to meet you I will tell you all about Sam if you like and I will introduce you to him. His name is "Sam the terrible." Not knowing what the future holds I shall say farewell and I will see you at the next job. Or should I say you will see my handiwork at the next job? Remember Ms. Lauria. Thank you. In their blood and from the gutter "Sam's creation" .44 Here are some names to help you along. Forward them to the inspector for use by N.C.I.C: "The Duke of Death" "The Wicked King Wicker" "The Twenty Two Disciples of Hell" "John 'Wheaties"—Rapist and Suffocator of Young Girls. PS: Please inform all the detectives working the slaying to remain. P.S: JB, Please inform all the detectives working the case that I wish them the best of luck. "Keep 'em digging, drive on, think positive, get off your butts, knock on coffins, etc." Upon my capture I promise to buy all the guys working the case a new pair of shoes if I can get up the money. Son of Sam.

The writer added an ominous postscript: "What will you have for July 29?" July 29 would be the one-year anniversary of the initial .44-caliber shooting. Would the Son of Sam celebrate the occasion with another attack?

Unlike the nonsensical, often illiterate letter sent to Captain Borrelli, this note was sophisticated in form and suggested a higher degree of education and intelligence. Police this time postulated that the author had a background in the arts, graphic design, or calligraphy.

Breslin was a hard-nosed veteran reporter with a gift for showing his readers how the news affected them personally. His column was a voice for the common man. Now, this gilt-edged reporter with the common voice held in his grasp the voice of an uncommon person.

After consulting with police, the *Daily News* one week later published an edited version of the letter; Breslin urged the killer to turn himself over to police. According to reports, that day's edition of the *News* sold more than one million copies. New Yorkers wanted to know what was happening in their neighborhoods. They needed to know what they could do to protect themselves from the Son of Sam.

They did what they needed to do in order to remain safe. Since all of the shooter's targets had long brown hair, many women donned blond wigs; others cut and dyed their hair. Beauty supply stores and stores that sold wigs were overwhelmed by demand. Supplies ran short, as did New Yorkers' patience with the investigation. In some neighborhoods, people formed their own posses, either to hunt for the killer or to protect their own families. Neighbors suspected neighbors; people of all ages and genders contacted the police with hundreds of tips. Not one was of real value. The summer of 1977 was one of the city's hottest and longest, and one of the quietest. The city that never sleeps was hibernating, and a killer was poised to strike.

The .44 Caliber Shooter did not wait for his one-year anniversary to arrive. He struck on June 26, 1977. This time, his victims survived, practically unscathed. Sal Lupo, age twenty, and Judy Placido, seventeen, had just concluded a night of dancing and partying at a Queens disco and were sitting in their car at about 3 A.M.

Placido said, "This Son of Sam is really scary—the way that guy comes out of nowhere. You never know where he'll hit next." Seconds later, Placido found out, as three gunshots slammed into the car. Lupo and Placido each were hit by slugs but sustained only minor injuries in the attack. Neither had spotted any suspicious persons in the area, but witnesses reported seeing a tall, stocky, dark-haired man running from the scene, plus a blond man with a mustache driving from the neighborhood in a Chevy Nova. The car's headlights were off. Police believed that the dark-haired man was the shooter, and the blond a witness to the shooting.

On July 28, Jimmy Breslin referenced the misspelled "wemon" in the author's letter. He also touched on the shooter's sense of alienation and desperation for attention "from his attic window." Breslin unwittingly was about to join the Son of Sam on New York's center stage.

With the one-year anniversary of the first shooting approaching, police focused their investigation on Queens and the Bronx, the sites of previous attacks. They established a dragnet around the shooter's favorite "hunting grounds" for attractive women with long brown hair. Undercover agents posed as women, parked conspicuously in cars, hoping to draw the .44 Caliber Shooter to them.

Their efforts failed. This time, the Son of Sam found his victims in Brooklyn. On July 31, 1977, Stacy Moskowitz and Robert Violante, both twenty, were sitting in his car, engaged in a passionate kiss. They were oblivious to their surroundings. And why not? Violante's car was parked near a neighborhood park, illuminated by a streetlight and full moon. They did not account for the shooter's desperation to carry out his nefarious mission, despite the threat of being seen. At around 2:35 A.M., a man emerged from the shadows and into the milky light. He approached the car as the lovers continued to embrace. He was just a few feet from the passenger's window when he opened fire, pummeling the car and its passengers with a barrage of bullets. The shooter fled into the pre-dawn darkness of the park. Hours later, Moskowitz was pronounced dead at a local hospital. Violante survived the attack, but a bullet had torn through one of his eyes and reduced vision in his other one.

This particular shooting especially worried police, for it precluded the shooter's previous modus operandi. Moskowitz, unlike the other female victims, had short blond hair. Also, the shooter had taken his murderous act beyond his previous hunting grounds, into Brooklyn. Now, neither blonds nor residents of other New York boroughs were safe.

Yet this shooting did produce more witnesses and clues than the others. Like Robert Violante, Tommy Zaino was enjoying a romantic evening with his date. They were parked in his car, some three car lengths ahead of Violante's vehicle. Unlike Violante, Zaino was not oblivious to life out on the street. Just seconds before the shots rang out, he noticed from the corner of his eye a figure moving toward Violante's car. Something prompted him to peer up and into his rearview mirror; the light cast by the moon and streetlight afforded Zaino an excellent view of the shooting. Zaino saw a man raise a gun and take aim at the passenger's side of the car: *Bang! Bang! Bang!*

Afterwards, Zaino described the perpetrator as between "25 and 30 years old, of average height (5'7" to 5'9"), with shaggy hair that was dark blonde or light brown—like a wig." For the description to match that of a man with dark, wiry hair, the shooter must have worn a disguise. Unless Son of Sam was not the killer this time.

Other witnesses provided more details, more pieces to this confusing, convoluted puzzle. From the other side of the park, a woman—also seated with her boyfriend in a car—spotted a "white male (who was wearing) a light-colored, cheap nylon wig" race from the park and hop into a vehicle she described as small and light in color. She watched the car speed away. In her description of the incident, the woman said, "He looks like he just robbed a bank." She recorded what she believed was the latter portion of the car's license plate: 4GUR or 4GVR. Other witnesses described a similar scene: the small car streaking from the site of the murder, some twenty seconds after shots were fired. At least two witnesses said they saw a yellow Volkswagen hurtle from the neighborhood, its headlights off. Another woman claimed to have seen a man, who later fit Berkowitz's description, saunter away from the shooting site as others raced to see what had happened.

Another man, whose identity was not disclosed by investigators, said he was driving through an intersection a few blocks from the shooting when a yellow Volkswagen nearly drove him off the road. The driver, according to this witness, was holding his door shut as he drove. The driver had a slender face, was in his twenties or thirties, had "long, stringy hair, several days' growth of dark whiskers on his face; and wearing a blue jacket." His curiosity piqued by the suspect's helter-skelter driving, the witness sped after the Volkswagen for several minutes before losing track of the car. The witness could not read the Volkswagen's license plate number, but he did believe it bore a New Jersey plate rather than a New York one.

The shooting produced another long night for New Yorkers, as well as a bevy of clues and witness statements, some of which contradicted each other. Descriptions of the shooter made some investigators wonder if this shooter was different from the previous one or ones. Only David Berkowitz knew the answer to that question.

Within an hour of the shooting, police had set up a series of roadblocks and were stopping hundreds of cars to question drivers and inspect vehicles. Extensive interviews with witnesses who described the yellow Volkswagen speeding from the scene suggested to police that the vehicle belonged to the shooter. In the first few days following the latest shooting, investigators learned that there were more than nine hundred Volkswagens in New York and New Jersey. They planned to contact the owner of each car. A daunting task, perhaps, but now police were one step closer to determining who the Son of Sam, the .44 Caliber Shooter, was.

The factors that led to Berkowitz's arrest were, to say the least, ironic. Initially, the NYPD pursued him as witness, and not as a suspect. On July 31, 1977, the night of the Moskowitz-Violante shooting, Cacilia Davis, who lived in the area of the shooting, spotted a man fitting Berkowitz's description, "loitering in the neighborhood and glaring menacingly as passersby for several hours before removing a parking ticket from his yellow Ford Galaxie." Police had given Berkowitz a ticket for parking too close to a fire hydrant. Berkowitz was now in a foul mood, whether from the ticket or from the demons telling him to kill. Whatever the reason, Berkowitz was angry enough to risk being identified by neighbors. His presence so disturbed Davis that she contacted police about this lingering, strange man.

On August 9, 1977, one week after Davis had called the police, NYPD detective James Justice called Yonkers police to set up a meeting with Berkowitz. Justice requested the aid of Yonkers police in tracking down Berkowitz. As fortune would have it, Justice spoke with a Yonkers sergeant named Mike Novotny. Novotny had investigated a series of other unusual crimes in the city and found references to the crimes in one of the Son of Sam letters. Novotny and the Yonkers PD agreed to help the NYPD. They thought Berkowitz just might be the Son of Sam, based on the letters, his experience in the military, his physical appearance, and the numerous acts of arson. Justice and his colleagues were stunned.

There was no time to waste. The following day, police drove to Berkowitz's Pine Street apartment in Yonkers. The located his car parked outside the apartment. In the backseat, they found a Commando Mark III rifle. They searched the car and found a duffel bag chock full of ammunition, maps of crime scenes, and a threatening letter addressed to Sgt. Dowd of the Omega Task Force. It was time to meet Mr. Berkowitz.

Rather than storm into the apartment building and raise a ruckus, police decided to wait outside for Berkowitz to emerge. At 10 P.M., he did just that, toting a .44 Bulldog. Police arrested him as he attempted to start his car. Berkowitz's reaction: "You got me. What took you so long?" Afterwards, police searched his apartment, which looked as psychotic as Berkowitz himself. Satanic graffiti adorned the walls, and the rooms were as upside down as Berkowitz's mind. In one of the rooms, investigators found Berkowitz's personal diary; in it, he claimed to have committed "dozens of arsons throughout the New York area."

With Berkowitz in police custody, Mayor Beame took control of the city's collective heart strings: "The people of the city of New York can rest easy," he declared publicly, "because of the fact that the police have captured a man whom they believe to be the Son of Sam." But did they legally have the Son of Sam in custody? Police had completed a search of Berkowitz's car without a search warrant. They justified their actions based on the rifle visible in the back seat. Yet possession of that rifle was legal in New York, without a special permit.

What happened next, however, made investigators' worries moot. Like George Metesky, the Mad Bomber, Berkowitz may have felt a deep-seated need to purge himself of the guilt associated with the killings. Maybe, like Metesky, he also wanted more public attention. Whatever the psychological basis for his subsequent actions, Berkowitz quickly, and shockingly, advised police he desired to confess to the murders in exchange for receiving a life sentence. A man so driven to kill was himself afraid of receiving the death penalty. On the morning of August 11, 1977, police sat down to extract a confession from David Berkowitz. Within a half hour, the suspect had confessed to all of the "Son of Sam" killings. He then gave a brief yet chilling explanation and motive for the murders: Harvey, the demon-possessed Labrador retriever, commanded Berkowitz's soul and had ordered him to kill.

If his confession chilled police, it equally shocked the jury convened to try Berkowitz for the murders. On June 12, 1978, he was sentenced to six life sentences in prison for the murders. He began the first of his 365 years in prison at Attica Correctional Facility, home of some of the most notorious and nefarious criminals in the nation's history.

The story should have ended there, but it merely bowed to a sequel that was equally yet paradoxically stunning. Just a few weeks after his arrest, Berkowitz began to suggest that he did not commit all of the .44 Caliber Shooter murders. In his letter to the *New York Post*, September 19, 1977, Berkowitz suggested New Yorkers may never be safe from a madman's gun: "There are other Sons out there, God help the world."

Years later, Berkowitz disclosed more of the modus operandi of his satanic cult, alleging that others in the clan had committed some of the murders. He was reluctant to discuss the group in detail, fearing retribution upon his family by extant cult members. He did say that the group was involved in "drug smuggling and other illegal activities." He referred to brothers John and Michael Carr, sons of Yonkers neighbor Sam Carr, as belonging to the cult. Berkowitz dubbed John Carr "John Wheaties, rapist and suffocater of young girls" as noted in the letter to Breslin. Ironically, the Carr brothers both died less than two years after Berkowitz's arrest. In February 1978, John Carr was found dead in the North Dakota home of his girlfriend. Police eventually ruled the death a "probable suicide." Michael Carr died in a traffic accident in October 1979 on Manhattan's West Side Highway. Berkowitz later postulated that the cult members probably murdered both men, who were heavy drug users and "likely to become informants."

Some members of the media had long believed more than one person was involved in the shootings. Then-NBC reporter John Hockenberry was one of the most vocal in questioning the "single gun" theory: "What most people don't know about the Son of Sam case is that from the beginning, not everyone bought the idea that Berkowitz acted alone. The list of skeptics includes both the police who worked the case and the prosecutor from Queens where five of the shootings took place."

Journalist Maury Terry is another skeptic of the single-shooter scenario. Terry began investigating the Son of Sam murders before Berkowitz's arrest and found a "number of unresolved questions and inconsistencies." He published his findings in a March 1978 newspaper article. Terry went on to interview Berkowitz several times, and he discovered evidence that supports a "violent offshoot of the Process Church." Terry argued that the members of this demonic splinter group were "responsible for the Son of Sam murders and many other crimes." Terry continued to publicize his findings in a series of 1979 newspaper articles for Gannett newspapers and then expanded his works into a book entitled *The Ultimate Evil*.

In 1979, FBI veteran Robert Ressler interviewed Berkowitz in depth. Berkowitz said he had invented the Son of Sam stories as a pretext for committing the murders. If caught, he argued, he could use the letters to show the court he was insane. Berkowitz claimed he killed because of the "resentment toward his mother and failures with women. He found killing to be sexually arousing."

Like many other reformed prisoners, including Connecticut's infamous serial killer Michael Ross, the Son of Sam discovered he was a Son of God while behind bars. According to his own personal reflections, Berkowitz transformed from the mouthpiece of Satan to a purveyor of the Lord's word in 1987. His moment of soul-shaking catharsis came after reading from the New Testament.

In 2002, he wrote then-New York governor George Pataki requesting the cancellation of his upcoming parole hearing: "In all honesty, I believe that I deserve to be in prison for the rest of my life. I have with God's help, long ago come to terms with my situation and I have accepted my punishment."

Once profoundly arrogant, he now appears to be humble. His penance, it seems, is ongoing. He receives dozens of letters each day from people seeking his help, guidance, and blessing. David Berkowitz, this reborn Son of God, has by most outward indications, changed from the inside out.

In June 2005, he sued his former attorney Hugo Harmatz, claiming he had taken possession of Berkowitz's letters and other personal belongings in order to publish a book of his own. On October, 25, 2006, the two settled out of court; Harmatz agreed to return the disputed items to Berkowitz's lawyer and to donate part of his book's profits to the New York State Crime Victims Board. The disagreement helped create new laws in New York preventing the criminal or others to benefit financially from book deals and the sale of other memorabilia. The "Son of Sam laws" give the state authorization to "seize all money earned from such a deal from a criminal for five years, with intentions to use the seized money to compensate victims."

More than thirty years have passed since David Berkowitz went on his killing spree, and the answer to this question remains ambiguous: Was David Berkowitz merely a madman, or did the Devil make him do it? Perhaps more chilling: What makes others think this purported born-again Christian and model inmate today is a prophet of God?

CHAPTER 5
Imagine There's No Heaven

Few killings in New York City history have been as personal as that of John Lennon. The December 8, 1980, death of the founding member of the Beatles, political activist, and icon affected many of us individually and was felt across the world.

Like his erstwhile hero, Lennon, Mark David Chapman had an ideal sense of how the world should operate. His views on himself, the world, and others were frequently ambivalent, often psychotic. In simplest terms, Chapman was a boy-man in search of attention, acceptance, and a hero whom he could emulate and follow.

It should come as no surprise that Chapman had an unhappy childhood; he lacked athleticism, which encouraged other boys to pick on him and call him derogatory names such as "Pussy." After being arrested for the murder of Lennon, Chapman told psychiatrists that he feared his father, who, Chapman claimed, beat his mother.

Chapman also said his father never gave him love or "the emotional support" he needed.

Those who knew David Chapman, Mark's father, recognized him as a solid member of the community, a Boy Scout troop leader who even taught guitar at the YMCA. Diane Chapman admitted later that her husband did strike her, but he also spent countless hours with his son in the yard playing ball.

In his article for the Tru TV Crime Library entitled "Mark David Chapman: The Man Who Killed John Lennon," Fred McGunagle quoted Diane Chapman describing her husband: "The fact is that Dave kept a darn good roof over our heads for all those years, and I would say he was a better parent to Mark than I was," she said. "It was true Dave didn't show his emotions, but he'd do anything for Mark."

Without the strong connection to society that he needed emotionally and psychologically, Chapman created his own fairy-tale world, consisting of made up characters and story lines. Author and reporter Jack Jones, who chronicled Chapman in his 1992 book *Let Me Take You Down: Inside the Mind of Mark David Chapman, the Man Who Killed John Lennon*, quotes Chapman: "I used to fantasize that I was a king, and I had all these Little People around me and that they lived in the walls. And that I was their hero and was in the paper every day and I was on TV every day, their TV, and that I was important. They all kind of worshipped me, you know. It was like I could do no wrong." Chapman desperately needed to be noticed and respected for something special. He enjoyed entertaining these "Little People" by performing one-man concerts with an accompanying record. More often than not, the Beatles' music was playing on his turntable.

Chapman also noted in Jones's book: "And sometimes when I'd get mad I'd blow some of them up. I'd have this push-button thing, part of the [sofa], and I'd like get mad and blow out part of the wall and a lot of them would die. But the people would still forgive me for that, and, you know, everything got back to normal. That's a fantasy I had for many years."

Although Chapman slowly disconnected from his family and the world as he grew up, most of the adults who knew him considered him a normal kid (with an IQ of 120) with interests such as rockets, UFOs, and music—especially the Beatles. Chapman enjoyed—perhaps even had a fantasy obsession with—Dorothy and the *Wizard of Oz*. He never missed the 1939 classic when it was aired. Unfortunately, Chapman's family and others in their inner circle missed Mark David Chapman's descent into a world of Little People and his emotional war between good and bad, Satan and God.

As a teenager growing up at Columbia High School in Decatur, Georgia, Chapman turned to marijuana, barbiturates, and heroin to deal with life. He grew his hair long and began to develop distinct antisocial traits: He defied his parents regularly, skipped school, and stayed out late at night. On one night he was so spaced-out on LSD that police had to rescue him and take him home. At least twice he ran away from home, once racing off to Miami where he spent two weeks living on the street. Finally, someone gave him enough money for him to buy a return bus ticket to Decatur. If anything was consistent in Chapman's behavior, it was his lack of emotional consistency.

After two years of drug dependency and self-alienation, Chapman found God. That is, he found an evangelist whose sermons moved him deep in his soul. The change in Chapman was almost immediate, and it was profound. He cut his long locks, scrubbed up his appearance, and wore a large wooden cross around his neck. He became a disciple of sorts, sowing the seeds of the Word, seeking ways to help himself and others. Gradually, Chapman's schoolwork, long neglected, improved. He became a summer camp counselor at a local YMCA summer camp; he even met a girl, Jessica Blankenship, also a born-again Christian.

Although he had long felt like a pariah, now he was sure he was someone important. And he was. Chapman was magnetic, and children—real "little people"—stuck to him and followed him wherever he went. Some of the kids even referred to Chapman as "Nemo," so named after the character in the Jules Verne book *20,000 Leagues*

Under the Sea. One year, this Nemo was named outstanding counselor at the camp, to a rousing chant of "Ne-mo, Ne-mo, Ne-mo!" from the kids.

At this stage in his life, Mark David Chapman loved the Lord and adored the Beatles, especially John Lennon. But he'd been bothered by a comment Lennon made in 1966, during an interview with Maureen Cleave of the *Evening Standard*: "Christianity will go. It will vanish and shrink. I needn't argue about that. I'm right and I will be proved right. We're more popular than Jesus now. I don't know which will go first—rock 'n roll or Christianity."

Who did Lennon think he was, Jesus Christ? Now, when Chapman and his Christian friends sang Lennon's anthem, "Imagine," they changed the words: "Imagine John Lennon is dead."

As significant as the Bible was to Chapman, the 1951 J. D. Salinger novel *The Catcher in the Rye* proved to be a map of Chapman's soul. The book, introduced to Chapman by school chum Michael McFarland, features a young man named Holden Caulfield. Like Chapman, Caulfield is in search of his place in the world, a world where his classmates and the adults in their lives appear to be phony and superficial. The protagonist Caulfield spends much of the book racing from place to place, person to person, seeking to fit in. The book contains themes with which Chapman was intimately familiar, and Caulfield was the "antihero" with whom Chapman would most identify over the next decade. But there was a problem: God's Word and Caulfield's words didn't always agree. It was just a matter of time before both powerful messages exploded inside Chapman's mind and soul.

For a while, the artistic, selfless, and nurturing side of Chapman's psyche shined. After graduating from high school, he joined McFarland in a Chicago-based variety show—Chapman played guitar and McFarland did standup comedy. The gig wasn't exactly a hit, and Chapman returned to Georgia, where he picked up a part-time job at a local YMCA and enrolled at South De Kalb Community College. He got his first real career break when the YMCA sent him to work in Lebanon as part of its summer international program. But civil unrest in the country forced the organization to relocate Chapman and other Y staffers to the U.S. Chapman drew an assignment working with Vietnamese refugees in Fort Chaffee, Arkansas. Once again, he seemed perfect for the job. He was named an area coordinator and demonstrated that he was as caring a person as he was hard a worker. But that resettlement camp lasted only about one year, and when Chapman left the college he was again looking to settle himself and his career. What he found was pain, guilt, and self-loathing.

Chapman followed Blankenship to Covenant College in Lookout Mountain, Tennessee, and enrolled. By this point, the couple had been discussing marriage. Covenant College, as the name might suggest, was a strict Presbyterian college. Chapman and Blankenship spent much of their time studying together and, naturally, discussing the Bible.

Doing so tormented Chapman, however. While working at the resettlement camp, Chapman had had an affair with a camp worker. Now, each moment he was with Blankenship, he was riddled with guilt. But he could not force himself to confess the affair to his girlfriend, who was still a virgin.

Harboring this growing remorse slowly forced Mark David Chapman back into his otherworld of demons and internal voices. His schoolwork began to suffer, and he was now haunted by feelings of failure—failing at the Y, failing in romance, failing his God. He became depressed, and over the next four years, he would be haunted by suicidal thoughts. He and Blankenship eventually broke up, and Chapman dropped out of college. He got an unsatisfying security guard job; he drifted, physically and emotionally.

Then he made a decision. In January 1977, Chapman took all of his $1,200 in savings and bought a one-way ticket to Hawaii, a nirvana for which he had pined for years. He planned to go to Honolulu, run free . . . and then kill himself.

After five days of living the high life of a tourist, he began to think about home, and about Blankenship. He thought about getting himself together and kick-starting his life. Come home, she told him. He did so in May of 1977, buying another one-way ticket, this time to Atlanta, with his remaining dollars and pennies. But the home to which he returned did not want him; that included his parents and Blankenship, who was more concerned about his mental stability than reigniting their relationship. With nowhere to go, Chapman bought another one-way ticket, this time back to Hawaii. With little money, Chapman ended up on the streets, making call upon call to suicide hot lines. He drank; there was no rescue from God now. No safe haven provided by Holden Caulfield. Mark David Chapman was alone.

Finally, despair overpowered Chapman. He rented a car and drove it to the beach. There, he hooked up a hose from the tailpipe and ran it back into the car. He turned on the car, allowing the poisonous fumes to seep back in. He slowly slipped into a dreamless unconsciousness. At that point, history could have changed—could have, that is, were it not for a Good Samaritan. A Japanese fisherman walked by the car and noticed that the hose had melted into the tailpipe. He tapped on the driver's side window.

"Are you alright?" he asked Chapman. Chapman slowly and groggily regained consciousness. When he did, the man was gone. But Chapman had gotten the message: God had sent an angel to save him, and Chapman would not let him down.

The following day, Chapman discussed his story with a psychiatrist at a nearby mental health clinic. Within hours, he had been admitted to Castle Memorial Hospital under suicide watch. But Chapman was anything but ready to take his life now. In fact, he recovered quickly, and soon he was entertaining other patients with songs and guitar solos. Soon after, the hospital discharged him, finding him a job at a nearby gas station. Chapman maintained a relationship with the hospital, the staff, and the patients; he volunteered there in his free time and eventually was hired as a maintenance person. By early 1978, he considered himself a success at work, with his coworkers, with the patients, and in life.

Still, there remained in him that little boy always dreaming of his own place—maybe in Nirvana? Maybe in a heaven that existed only in his mind? Whatever the case, after running off to Hawaii, Chapman now dreamed of flying off to the Far East. Though whimsical, Chapman nevertheless was pragmatic. He borrowed money from the hospital credit union and began to make plans for a six-week around-the-world adventure. He arranged the trip with a Japanese-American travel agent named Gloria Abe. And then a funny thing happened. He fell for Gloria.

Upon returning from overseas, Chapman started up a romance with Gloria. He encouraged her to convert from Buddhism to Christianity, which she did. In January 1979, while the couple walked along the beach, Chapman wrote in the sand: "Will you marry me?" She wrote back, "Yes." They set a wedding date of June 2.

It seemed as if Chapman was one small step shy of entering his nirvana. Then he made a decision that would forever change his life. Seeking to earn some extra money before the wedding, Chapman added a second job as a printer at Castle Memorial. Unlike his other jobs at the hospital, where he was constantly surrounded by others and was, for all intents and purposes an icon, now he worked alone. Solitude. No one there to remind him of his greatness. Soon, the job and the loneliness began to eat away at his soul. He grew angry, almost violently so. His temper cost him his job and Gloria hers.

He went through a cycle of obsessive behavior—first buying expensive artwork, and then scrimping and saving to get out of debt with Gloria, now his wife. By the spring of 1980, he was back on an emotional roller coaster. The voices of those pesky Little People were back, shouting directions at him. And soon, so was Holden Caulfield.

That summer, Chapman bought two copies of *The Catcher in the Rye*. He made Gloria read the book. He told her he was thinking of changing his name to Holden Caulfield; he even researched how to do so.

According to McGunagle, Chapman on September 20 "wrote a letter to a friend, Lynda Irish, in New Mexico. On it he drew a picture of Diamond Head with the sun, moon and stars above it. 'I'm going nuts,' he wrote. He signed it 'The Catcher in the Rye.'"

Amidst this particular fantasy, another voice reentered Chapman's conscience—John Lennon's. Remembering how Lennon had put the Beatles on the same scale as Jesus, Chapman began to research John Lennon's life. What made Lennon tick? Ultimately, Chapman's research led him to this painful question: How could a man who preached peace and simplicity live in the proverbial lap of luxury while others struggled in poverty? Was Lennon no better than the "phonies" in *Catcher in the Rye*? Chapman wondered.

By now, Chapman's Little People had developed into an ersatz board of counselors that had their own itinerary and suggested it vigorously to Chapman. He told them he wanted to kill John Lennon. The Little People begged him to reconsider. Chapman would not. Jones explained in his book: "One by one, beginning with his defense minister, the Little People rose from their seats and walked from the secret chamber inside the mysterious mind of Mark David Chapman."

What followed happened quickly and seemingly without Chapman's ability to control it. In October, shortly after Lennon and Yoko Ono released their album *Double Fantasy*, Chapman purchased a five-shot short barrel, a .38-caliber Charter Arms Special, for $139 with the remaining money of an earlier $5,000 loan from his father-in-law. Chapman left his wife and his home. His destination, New York City. His target, John Lennon.

After arriving in "the City that Never Sleeps," Chapman checked into the ritzy Waldorf and finalized his plans for Lennon's murder. Chapman, like many other New Yorkers, knew that numerous celebrities lived in the Dakota apartment hotel, across from Central Park at West 72nd Street. Chapman spent an entire day studying the layout and geography of the building and the street. He searched out Lennon's sixth-floor windows. Were they home? He wondered. Presenting himself as a stereotypical fan, he asked a doorman at the building if John and Yoko were in town. The doorman did not know.

Chapman was prepared to conduct day-long vigils in order to catch Lennon. He made plans to do so. In what could be best described as a tactical error, however, Chapman had not purchased bullets for the gun before coming to New York. He soon discovered that because of the state's Sullivan laws, he could not purchase .38-caliber bullets.

Ever resourceful, Chapman contacted an old friend, Dana Reeves, in Atlanta. Reeves was now a sheriff's deputy and Chapman figured that Reeves could set him up with the ammo he needed. Chapman flew to Atlanta, under the guise of wanting to reestablish ties with old friends. When he arrived at Reeves's home, Chapman pleaded for protection while in New York, as well as requesting hollow-point rounds for his gun.

There were many signposts in Mark David Chapman's road map of life, emotional clues that directed him how to behave. After returning to New York on November 10, Chapman went to see the Academy Award-winning movie *Ordinary People*, the story of a "suicidal youth trying to come to terms with his dysfunctional family." Again, Chapman found himself identifying with an outcast. Shortly after the movie, Chapman called Gloria at home. He told her he had "won a great victory and that . . . her love had saved him."

But had it? Shortly after returning to Hawaii, Chapman resumed his bizarre behavior. He made threatening phone calls to strangers, bomb threats to others. According to published reports, Chapman even spent hours at a time tormenting a group of Hare Krishnas who met daily in downtown Honolulu. Like many observers, Gloria was shocked by his behavior. Yet she did not leave him. Finally, the demons in Chapman's soul chased him back to hell—New York City. It was December 6, 1980.

This time, Chapman lived frugally, staying in a YMCA near Central Park. He was just nine blocks from the Dakota, so logistically, he was in better position to cross paths with Lennon. Nevertheless, he changed his mind and, the next day, he checked out of the Y and into the Sheraton Centre at Seventh Avenue and 52nd

Street. It was, ironically, Pearl Harbor Day, and Mark David Chapman was ready to attack—if Lennon would just appear.

Chapman spent a few hours that day staking out the Dakota. No sign of Lennon. Finally, frustrated and hungry, he took a taxi back to the hotel, stopping at a bookstore to pick up another copy of *Catcher in the Rye*, since he'd left his copy at home. Instead, he bought a poster of Oz's Dorothy with the Cowardly Lion. He also nabbed a copy of the new *Playboy*, which contained an interview with John and Yoko Ono. After returning to the hotel, he devoured the article as ravenously as he did his dinner. Afterwards, he emulated Holden Caulfield by contacting an escort service; like Caulfield, Chapman and the call girl merely talked. Chapman paid her $190 for her listening skills.

On December 8, 1980, Chapman awoke to his world of paradoxes. Sensing today was the day he would complete his mission, he blessed himself by opening the Bible to the Gospel of John. Chapman then penned in the word "Lennon" after the word "John." To further steel himself, he reviewed a letter of thanks for his work at the Vietnamese refugee camp. With the letter were snapshots of him with Vietnamese children. Included in his assortment of good luck charms was the poster of Dorothy and the Cowardly Lion.

Mark David Chapman now had the courage he needed to stalk and kill John Lennon. En route to the Dakota, Chapman picked up another copy of the Bible and one of *The Catcher in the Rye*. On the inside cover, he wrote, "this is my statement, Holden Caulfield."

Then Chapman returned to the Dakota and continued his vigil. Caught up in reading *The Catcher*, he missed Lennon's arrival by taxi at the hotel. He did eventually meet Sean Lennon, John's five-year-old son. And for a moment, the sane and loving side of Chapman reemerged. James R. Gaines described the moment in a three-part story he wrote on Chapman for *People* magazine, in 1987:

> He was the cutest little boy I ever saw. It didn't enter my mind that
> I was going to kill this poor young boy's father and he won't have

a father for the rest of his life. I mean, I love children. I'm the Catcher in the Rye.

Chapman also saw a host of celebrities pass by. Finally, the waiting paid off: He spotted Lennon and Yoko Ono leaving the building, trailed by members of their staff. Shocked beyond speech, Chapman could merely stick out the "Double Fantasy" record album and a pen. Lennon, renowned for his graciousness toward his fans, smiled and signed the cover, "John Lennon, December 1980." Chapman described the meeting ten years later on Court TV's *Mugshots.*

> He said "Sure" and wrote his name, and when he handed it back to me he looked at me and kind of nodded his head, "Is that all you want?"
>
> Like just like that, like an inquiry into a different matter, and I said, "Yeah." I said, "Thanks, John."
>
> And he again said, "Is that all you want?" and there was Yoko, she was already in the car, the limo, the door was open and it was running, it was out in the middle of the street and he asked me twice, and I said, "Yeah, thanks, that's all," or something like that. He got into the car and drove away.

Chapman's feelings of ambivalence toward his icon/enemy underscored his paradoxical God-Satan-driven psyche. When you met him, Lennon seemed down-to-earth, Chapman thought. He told Gaines: "I was just overwhelmed by his sincerity. I had expected a brush-off, but it was just the opposite. I was on Cloud Nine. And there was a little bit of me going, 'Why didn't you shoot him?' And I said, 'I can't shoot him like this.' I wanted to get the autograph."

As Lennon departed, Chapman had in one hand the signed album and in his pocket, the gun he would use to shoot Lennon. At that moment, Mark David Chapman prayed to God for the strength to walk away.

Demons come, but demons never really go away—at least, not Chapman's. He remained at the Dakota throughout the day and into night. At 10:50 P.M. Lennon and Yoko Ono returned to the Dakota in a white limousine. Yoko emerged first. Chapman later recounted the shooting in his statement to police:

> He walked past me, and then a voice in my head said, "Do it, do it, do it," over and over again, saying "Do it, do it, do it, do it," like that.
>
> I pulled the gun out of my pocket, I handed over to my left hand, I don't remember aiming, I must have done it, but I don't remember drawing the bead or whatever you call it. And I just pulled the trigger steady five times.

Chapman was in a shooter's position when he fired six shots. Lennon's back was to him. Four of the shots slammed into Lennon's body; somehow, none of the bullets struck Yoko.

"I'm shot," cried Lennon. Then he collapsed

Mortally wounded, Lennon was helped up the stairs to the Dakota security office as an agitated Chapman waved the gun in the air, shouted warnings at bystanders, and paced back and forth anxiously. Doorman Jose Perdomo turned to him: "Do you know what you done? Do you know what you done!" Perdomo slapped the gun out of Chapman's hand and kicked it out of harm's way.

Finally, Chapman began to calm down. Perhaps he was numb with shock; maybe he was satisfied that he had completed his mission. Whatever the case, he made no effort to run. Eventually, he calmly picked up his copy of the *The Catcher in the Rye* and began to read. He waited for the police to arrive.

Two uniformed cops were the first to arrive in a cruiser. The first officer raced inside the apartment building. Perdomo stopped the other, and cited Chapman.

"Don't hurt me," Chapman cried. "I'm unarmed."

Officer Stephen Spiro spread-eagled Chapman and searched him. "I acted alone," said Chapman. Spiro then arrested Chapman and confiscated a .38-caliber snub-nosed revolver. The police then handcuffed Chapman and put him in the police car.

"I'm sorry I gave you guys all this trouble," he kept telling them.

Meanwhile police carried the ailing Lennon down to a waiting patrol and raced off to Roosevelt Hospital. During the brief ride, a hysterical Yoko pleaded with police, "Tell me it isn't true!"

During the transport of both Lennon and Chapman, Alan Weiss lay in the emergency room at Roosevelt Hospital in New York City. A news producer at WABC-TV in New York, Weiss often drove past the Dakota en route to the television station. He was a big Beatles fan, a devotee of Lennon and his music. As fate would have it, Weiss would get as close to the dying icon as any man in the city.

While riding his motorcycle to work, Weiss collided with a taxi as he emerged from Central Park on 59th Street at Seventh Avenue. Since he was just crossing the park, Weiss had neglected to buckle his helmet. He slammed into the taxi at 30 miles per hour, cracked the windshield, and skittered off the car and into the street. When his body hit the pavement, Weiss's helmet flew off. He slammed his head at least twice against the pavement before rolling to a halt.

Now, in great pain, he awaited treatment. In Larry Kane's book *Lennon Revealed*, Weiss describes the surreal scene when the dying Lennon arrived at the hospital:

I'm lying in the gurney, the doctor comes over, and she indeed is beautiful, and she looks at me and says, "You know, I'll take you in for x-rays. I have to see what's wrong with you." I said, "Fine." She says, "You're lucky. We're slow tonight." She had no sooner said that and all of a sudden a man comes in screaming, "We have a gunshot, we have a gunshot! Gunshot in the chest!" And she says, "When's he coming in?" "Hitting the door right now!" And the door slams open. Six cops come running in with a stretcher between them. And she looks at me and says, "Alan, I'm sorry. I gotta take care of this." So I'm lying there on the gurney and these guys run right into the room and I'm lying outside of it. So I'm lying there, my eyes are closed, two cops come out and one says to the other, "Jesus, can you believe it? John Lennon." And I open my eyes and I look up at these two cops standing over my bed and I said, "I'm sorry sir. What did you say?" They walk away and . . . now people are flying in and out of this room and they're carrying blood, gauze, and all sorts of other things and I'm trying to speak to them saying, "Excuse me. Who's in there?" And no one will talk to me.

And I hear crying and I look up and there is an Asian looking woman in a full-length mink coat on the arm of this huge motorcycle-jacketed police officer coming in. I don't know if that's gotta be Yoko Ono. It's gotta be John Lennon. So I realized that I had to get up and make a phone call and so, maybe the adrenalin starts flowing, suddenly the injury disappears.

Weiss hopped down the hallway in search of a pay phone. He had to call the newsroom. He spotted a pay phone outside of a glass door. He headed for the door. Suddenly, a security guard intercepted him. "You can't leave," he said. Weiss argued that it was a public place and he had the right to leave. *You cannot leave*, the guard repeated. Finally, the disagreement, increasing in volume, caught the attention of another cop, the officer who had initially transported Weiss to the ER.

"What are you doing up?" he asked Weiss.

"Didn't you hear?" said Weiss.

"Didn't we hear what?" said the cop.

"Didn't you hear that John Lennon's been shot?"

The cop looked at Weiss as if he were nuts. He reminded him that he had banged his head a couple of times. Weiss continued to argue. "Let me call my office," he told the officer. Finally, the cop gave in and handed Weiss a phone from the nursing stand. Weiss called his producer back at WABC-TV.

I'm sitting on the edge of my gurney watching them working on John Lennon inside the room. And he's stark naked and his legs are facing me, and there were doctors and stuff was hanging out . . .I could see his chest. To me his chest looked open; I could be wrong. It might have just been that there was blood on his chest. They were clearly working on him.

Moments later, Weiss was wheeled out of the emergency room and into an adjacent room. He heard music wafting gently from the hospital sound system: "All My Loving" or "Till There Was You"— one of the Beatles songs was playing. At the moment, Weiss wasn't sure which it was. Then, a few short yet interminable minutes later, Weiss heard a woman's screams: "No! No! Oh, NO!" A door opened. Yoko Ono emerged, sobbing uncontrollably, supported by record executive David Geffen.

Weiss told his producer, "They walked down the hall together . . . and it was . . . sadly . . . over."

Perhaps writer Pete Hamill summed up the death of John Lennon most eloquently in this quote from his *New York* magazine article:

"At the morgue, the entrance was sealed shut with a lock and chain. Attendants in green mortuary masks moved around in dumb show, their words inaudible, or typed on forms on grim civil-service typewriters. Behind them, in a refrigerator, lay the sixties."

The music died on December 9, 1980, but life went on. Against the advice of his lawyer, Chapman pleaded guilty to second-degree murder. He was sentenced to a prison term of twenty years to life, and he remains behind bars at Attica State Prison in New York.

CHAPTER 6
The Boss of Bosses Falls

"Angelo, what does Cosa Nostra mean? Cosa Nostra means that the boss is your boss. You understand? Forget about all this nonsense." —Gambino family wiseguy John Gotti advising fellow mobster Angelo "Quack Quack" Ruggiero to obey boss Paul Castellano.

Don't ever cross your boss, John Gotti told Angelo Ruggiero. Unless, of course, your boss crosses you and your family. Then, Gotti knew, if you had the balls and the smarts and the support of others, you could do whatever you wanted.

By the end of 1985, John Gotti was not only a man of strength, power, and muscle, he was a visionary who knew how to get his way with salesmanship and finesse as well as with a gun. And when he, like Angelo Ruggiero, decided that their boss Paul Castellano no longer merited running the Gambino crime family, Gotti acted with vision, precision, and speed.

73

December 16, 1985. A chilly, clear afternoon in New York City. It's the middle of rush hour, as shoppers race pell-mell through the streets, seeking the best bargains in this holiday season. There's an air of anticipation sweeping through the middle of Manhattan, as thousands of city-goers throng the streets, oblivious to each other. Amidst this typical mayhem, no one notices a black Lincoln Continental glide into an open space outside of Sparks Steak House. No one, that is, except John Gotti, soon to become one of the Mafia's and New York's most infamous gangsters. After the car stops, a tall, robust man impeccably dressed in a business suit and overcoat emerges from the car. His style, carriage, somber countenance, and prominent beak-like nose identify him; he is Paul Castellano, king of the Gambino crime family, Boss of the Bosses, the top don among New York's underworld families.

Castellano, a beefy man who enjoys the finest cuts of beef, is a regular at Sparks, which specializes in steaks. Tonight's engagement includes dinner and business, and Castellano is prepared for both. He is not ready, however, to defend himself. His underboss and driver, Thomas Bilotti, is unarmed, and Castellano has no other security force to protect him from what happens next. Before Castellano has a chance to shut the car door, gunshots shear through the noisy hubbub of the city, cutting down the don. Another round of shots rings through the night, and Bilotti, like his boss, is fatally wounded. Amidst the happy Christmas shoppers, the bodies of Castellano and Bilotti lie on the pavement for all to see.

From a nearby car, the man who hired the hit, John Gotti, watches this surreal scene with fellow Gambino member Sammy "The Bull" Gravano. They cruise slowly from the scene of the shooting. The man who had blocked Gotti's ascension through the ranks of the Gambino family was no more, and the landscape and modus operandi of the famous Gambino family, and New York Mafia, is about to change. Paul Castellano's forward-thinking efforts to legitimize the Gambino family and its business operations had cost him the respect and honor of old-school Mob thugs such as Gotti. His methodology had now cost him his life and had given John Gotti the opportunity to return the family to its glory days.

Castellano's death, in retrospect, was ironic, since he died in such a violent and public manner. During his reign as the head of New York's most powerful crime family, Big Paul was anything but ostentatious or socially comfortable. He preferred to work out of the public eye and was deeply concerned about the appearance he and his rank and file demonstrated in the business and public realms. Castellano dressed in fine, conservatively tailored suits that allowed him to blend in among New York's masses. At home he was the sophisticated business magnate, frequently dressed in "satin and silk dressing gowns and velvet slippers." He preferred briefcases, dialogue, and standard business agreements to firearms and physical violence—though he was not afraid to push the button when circumstances so demanded.

He commiserated with and sought counsel from a handful of high-ranking associates, and he had little involvement with his lower ranking confederates and soldiers. Castellano was, in a world of anti-social, psychotic personalities, aloof and atypical. His inability to connect to the old-school pulse and ways of his family ultimately perpetrated his undoing. To some members of the family, especially Gotti, Castellano had no business even running the Gambino family. Gotti was—based on traditional Mob law and the rationale of Castellano's dissenters—correct.

Born in 1915, Constantino Paul Castellano came into the world as he departed—his blood belonging to the Mob and his taste buds to beef. Paul's father Giuseppe was a butcher and a member of the Mangano crime family, predecessor of the Gambino family. The Castellano family helped to sponsor the arrival of Carlo Gambino to the U.S. in 1921. It didn't take long for Paul to put down roots both in the meat industry and in the Mangano family. At age nineteen, he was arrested but refused to divulge to police the names of his accomplices. As a result, he served a three-month prison term. Higher-ups in the Mangano regime noted young Castellano's loyalty to the family. That loyalty, however, would come into question during Castellano's final years.

Castellano became a full-fledged member of the Mangano Family in the 1940s, rising to the rank of capo. But as he matured and gained business experience, Paul Castellano focused more on trimming the fat off a porterhouse steak than from an opposing family's flank. Utilizing his pedigree in the meat industry and his Mob connections, Castellano opened a wholesale poultry distribution business that was a wild success. At its height, Castellano supplied meat to more than three hundred butchers in New York City. Mega food chains Key Food and Waldbaums in time became two of his premier customers.

Castellano's entry into the murder market was equally strange, and it came in 1975. The victim was the boyfriend of Castellano's daughter. Big Paul ordered the hit after learning that the man spouted that Castellano (and his hawkish nose) resembled Frank Perdue, chairman and spokesperson for the well-known poultry company. Perdue, the balding, amiable owner of the company, boasted that his own remarkable proboscis and visage looked like those of the birds he raised. Typical of his unpredictability, Castellano later lent his support to Perdue, who was having trouble with union squabbles at one of his processing plants. Perdue would rue the association for years to come.

With his businesses thriving, Castellano got what appeared to be his break with the Gambino crime family. With Don Carlo Gambino's health declining, Castellano was appointed acting boss. With Gambino's death the following year, Castellano assumed the role officially.

But what seemed like the opportunity of a lifetime was fraught with peril and slow but impending doom. Loyalty and honor are two of the cornerstones of a Mob family. Castellano's appointment to the head of the Gambino family shook the cornerstones, for Castellano was not technically in line for the job. According to family hierarchy, underboss Aniello "Neil" Dellacroce should have been elevated to the don. However, according to legend, before his death Gambino had tagged Castellano as his successor. The Castellano family of Sicily was chiefly responsible for bringing Carlo Gambino to the United States. Gambino had married Castellano's sister and wished to keep "Gambino blood" atop the family organization. Dellacroce was disappointed but stayed loyal to Castellano and the Gambino clan. Nevertheless, Carlo Gambino had set in motion the events that would lead to Big Paul's demise.

But Paul Castellano was more interested in building a legitimate business empire than he was in dealing with what he considered petty family squabbles. He took pride in his business success and envisioned the day when the Gambino family and its business operations would be completely legitimate. Castellano took pride in his negotiating skills—both in the meat business and in Mob deliberations.

With Castellano at the helm, the Gambino family tightened and expanded its grip on the building industry. For years, it had in its pocket Teamsters Local 282, "which could literally bring most construction jobs in New York to a halt." Castellano's influence reached as far as Kuwait.

As a businessman, Castellano also was concerned with the impression he created in the world. Castellano was reserved, almost proper, if such a description could be applied to a man whose job was to order others to slaughter meat and human beings. He ate well, dressed well, and was publicly soft-spoken. His home, a stately mansion dubbed "The White House" in the ritzy Todt Hill section of Staten Island, underscored his bent for propriety and sophistication. Such hallmarks of his character would quickly distance Castellano from the "gauche" underlings who spoke in simple sentences punctuated with .44-caliber bullets. Old-school "Mustache Petes" such as Dellacroce and up-and-comers such as Gotti railed against Castellano's forward-thinking, monarchial way of doing business.

Castellano, a man of contradictions, was not without traditional Mob blood running through his veins. When necessary he used force to ensure his family's noble, proper image. When Nicholas

Scibetta, Gravano's imprudent brother-in-law, engaged in activities considered "embarrassing to the family," Castellano had him killed. To protect himself and his interests in Brooklyn, Castellano surrounded himself with gangs that could scare the life out of the Grim Reaper himself.

He established a working relationship with a group of Irish-American mobsters known as the "Westies." The Westies, from Hell's Kitchen, served as Castellano's "enforcers and hitters," when violence was the meal of the day. Castellano also kept up ties with a network of Sicilians known as the Cherry Hill Gambinos; this association imported and distributed massive quantities of heroin throughout the U.S., at a time when drug dealing was a key industry for many New York families (Castellano prohibited his family members from dealing in narcotics). Most frightening was the crew headed by capo Roy DeMeo. DeMeo, like his boss, was a skilled butcher, and even more skilled at carving human beings into flank steaks. Authors Gene Mustain and Jerry Capeci wrote in their book *Murder Machine* that DeMeo's gang "specialized in draining the blood from bodies, cutting them up into small pieces, wrapping the pieces into small packages, and disposing of them so they wouldn't be found." They hung out regularly at the Gemini Lounge, where one of DeMeo's cousins, Joseph "Dracula" Guglielmo, and dozens of people were known to have met their end. Dellacroce's "muscle" may have lacked the color and violence of the DeMeo gang, but the clan boasted an up-and-comer who soon became Castellano's chief nemesis—John Gotti.

By the end of the 1970s, members of the Gambino family began to express privately their dissatisfaction with Castellano and his standoffish ways. Many "wiseguys" pointed to Castellano's emphasis on mainstream business, his very public mansion, and his very impersonal way of dealing with even his closest associates within the organization. Castellano rarely interacted with his foot soldiers, despite demanding tributes from them, and preferred to keep close ties with a trustworthy group of capos: Thomas "Tommy" Gambino,

Daniel "Danny" Marino, James "Jimmy Brown" Failla, Thomas "Tommy The Rug" Bilotti, and John "Uncle Johnny" Perrillo.

Castellano's business paradigm differed from those in the rank and file who preferred the old-school method of doing business. Big Paul sought to further the tactics utilized by Gambino, taking money earned from illegal operations and investing it in legitimate ventures. Castellano's confederates were involved in high-level extortion and other white collar crimes, such as bribery, construction, waste management, and the garment industry. Dellacroce's crews preferred "blue collar crime," including the rackets, extortion, drug trafficking, prostitution, loan sharking, and hijacking. Those loyal to Dellacroce worried that if the family went legitimate, there'd be no room for the criminal elements and workhorse crews who did the dirty work. No one was more acutely aware of this schism than Dellacroce's protégé, John Gotti.

By 1980, the fabric of the Gambino family was beginning to tear, and a few family members were overtly operating against Castellano's ways. Castellano, despite his alliances with groups that did traffic drugs, was adamantly against his family members moving narcotics. He made his feelings clear: You sell drugs, you die. Castellano so condemned the drug trade that he made a deal with Genovese family crime boss Vincent "Chin" Gigante to "execute, without warning or appeal, any member caught dealing drugs." Many of the Gambino family's wiseguys—including John Gotti—made a comfortable living dealing dope. Castellano's insistence on prosecuting his family's drug dealers underscored his disconnection with the family's ways and means.

Yet as Castellano fought for control over his Mob family, he neglected to control the most important person in the Gambino family—himself. Castellano's $3.5 million mansion high up in a ritzy Staten Island enclave bore a moderate resemblance to the White House, and Castellano believed he could operate therein with impunity. He was the Boss of all Bosses, after all, over his wife, as well as his Columbian maid, Gloria Orlate. But Castellano's troops were further incensed when they heard rumors that Castellano was having an affair with Orlate while he remained married. Today, many experts believe that Orlate had a hand in enabling the feds in 1983 to plant bugs in the White House. In fact, the FBI garnered hundreds of hours of recorded dialogue—much of it regarding illegal activities—between Castellano and his underlings. Their recordings also caught Big Paul flirting with the maid. Joseph F. O'Brien and Andrew Kurins were two of the agents responsible for planting the listening devices. In their book, *The Fall of the Godfather: The FBI and Paul Castellano*, the agents write that Castellano "doted on (Orlate) . . . Like adolescents . . . the pair indulged in long sessions of kissing and petting, stroking and teasing without ever having

MOB NICKNAMES

Practically since there have been wiseguys, there have been wise nicknames for mobsters: "Tony the Ant," "Joey the Clown," "Joe Batters." Such snappy monikers help to distinguish the Mafioso, often magnifying a unique physical trait, style, job description, or biological name. Many nicknames were assigned by neighborhood pals; others were plugged atop newspaper articles by overzealous headline writers keen on selling newspapers. Whatever its roots, each nickname tells a story about the gangster.

Paul Castellano was called the "Boss of Bosses" because he was believed to wield the most power of the five New York Families during his reign atop the Gambino crime family. His successor, John Gotti, was dubbed "The Dapper Don" by the media, primarily because of the snappy, custom-tailored suits he wore. He also became known as "The Teflon Don" because of his acquittal in three separate trials in the late 1980s.

Charlie Luciano got the name "Lucky" after surviving a vicious beating and knifing from a local rival. He emerged with his badge of life—a scar that ran down his cheek and gave him a look of rugged invincibility.

actual intercourse." In perhaps his most glaring act of vanity, Castellano later underwent surgery "to regain his sexual prowess for her."

To many of his rank and file, Castellano's lifestyle and business style were an embarrassment to the family. Perhaps no wise guy disdained Castellano's behavior more than John Gotti. Gotti's ire with the don was reaching a boiling point.

As the 1980s unfolded, Castellano's "sloppiness" and the FBI's improved tactics and surveillance methods helped to bring down Big Paul. In 1982 Castellano was indicted along with capo Roy DeMeo in a stolen luxury car ring. According to investigative reporter Selwyn Raab, "the indictment in Manhattan charged that the ring stole and shipped hundreds of luxury model cars to Kuwait, clearing

Nicholas Virgilio was the bodyguard for ex-Philadelphia boss Nicky Scarfo. Scarfo was more affectionately referred to as "Nick the Blade" because, as one gangster put it, "his first line of defense was hacking away at you with a knife." (His son is known as "Nick the Pen Knife.")

Other monikers relate to a special incident in the thug's life. In 2001, *Philadelphia Daily News* staff writers Jim Nolan and Kitty Caparella recounted the tale of how mobster Steve "Snitch" Frangipani allegedly got his nickname. A Mob associate and cargo thief, Frangipani had already pleaded guilty in the racketeering case against Joseph "Skinny Joey" Merlino and six others. The Snitch was not the kind of guy you trusted, if you believe every name defines a mobster's ideals and methods. According to Nolan and Caparella, law enforcement sources said that Frangipani got tagged with the nickname when he was in elementary school. When his teacher asked Frangipani to complete a task, Frangipani squealed on one of his classmates.

Mobster-turned-informer Sammy Gravano earned the moniker "Sammy the Bull" when he was a child growing up in Brooklyn. One day, two larger boys attempted to steal Gravano's bicycle. Though smaller than each of his assailants, Gravano fought and clawed recklessly and fearlessly until the bullies gave up. As a mobster, Gravano took part in nine-

(continued on page 82)

teen murders before testifying against his don, John Gotti, and escaping the underworld through the FBI's Witness Protection program.

Anthony Accardo earned the respect of Al Capone and the nickname "Joe Batters" after knocking two guys out of the park with a Louisville Slugger. Capone noted afterwards, "This kid is a real joe batters." Ironically, that moniker failed to stick with the press, who coined their own nickname for Accardo, "Big Tuna," after finding a snapshot of him fishing.

Some names are as obvious as the hawklike beaks on gangsters' faces: Vincent "Chin" Gigante's moniker is an abbreviation of his real name, Vincenzo. Curiously, the New York mobster was so frightened of being publicly addressed that he demanded people rub their chins when referring to him, rather than calling his name.

Gaeton "Horsehead" Scafidi was not known for stuffing a prized stallion's severed head into an enemy's bed. The horsehead was his own head, which was enormous, with a long sloping face that made him look like a contender in the Kentucky Derby. The nickname, comically, was assigned to him in the third grade.

Legend has it that Mafia capo Peter "Pete the Crumb" Caprio earned his nickname because he was "crumby-looking," as in wearing the remnants of his lunch.

Perhaps the least likely moniker went to Chicago Mob boss "Joey the Clown" Lombardo. Well known for his silliness and mostly unfunny jokes,

$5,000 on every sedan. Castellano was said to have received $20,000 in a wad of one-hundred-dollar bills every week as his share of the profits, though it was unlikely that he had a direct hand in the crew's operation and the twenty-five murders linked to it."

In January 1983, DeMeo's body was found stuffed into the trunk of his Cadillac; he'd been shot numerous times behind each ear. Castellano was arrested on March 30, 1984, and charged with ordering the murders of twenty-four people, a charge corroborated by information garnered from wire taps in his home. He was released on $2 million bond.

Lombardo earned the clown nickname from the press. At the conclusion of one of his trials, Lombardo sought to avoid public attention by fashioning a newspaper mask, complete with eyeholes.

In his December 13, 1987, article, *New York Times* reporter Arnold H. Lubasch underscored the priceless value of a gangster's nickname in the following dialogue between Anthony "Fat Tony" Salerno and Matthew "Matty the Horse" Ianniello. At the time, they were on trial and charged with being leaders of the Genovese crime family. The pair was discussing Bonanno family kingpin Philip "Rusty" Rastelli, who was considering inducting new members into the crime family.

"Rusty—he wanted to know if it's O.K. to make these guys," Mr. Ianniello said to Mr. Salerno. "He gave me a list."

"I don't know none of them," Mr. Salerno complained after looking at the list. "They don't put the nicknames down there."

"They should have the nicknames down," Mr. Ianniello agreed in the discussion, which was presented as evidence in the trial in Federal court. "Rusty wants to make sure he don't put nobody in there that a guy has got something against."

As Shakespeare once wrote, "What's in a name?"

Although Castellano and his closest associates were confident that the prosecution's case would not hold up, the don prepared a business course for his successor, should he, Castellano, be imprisoned. He chose Thomas Gambino, son of the late, great Carlo Gambino, with Thomas Bilotti, then a capo, serving as underboss. When the pro-Dellacroce Manhattan clan learned of Castellano's intentions, they fumed. First, Dellacroce and many others in the family feared that Castellano might crack and make a deal with the feds in order to avoid imprisonment. Worse yet, the Manhattan crew considered Thomas Gambino more "white collar" than

Castellano, and Bilotti was nothing more than Castellano's chauffeur and bodyguard.

On February 25, 1985, Castellano was arrested on charges of racketeering in the Mob-controlled construction business. Using information garnered by the FBI, United States Attorney Rudolph Giuliani, under the Racketeer Influenced and Corrupt Organizations Act (RICO), indicted eleven underworld members, including the five heads of the New York Families. Feds charged thirteen members of the Gambino crime family with drug trafficking. Among those charged were Gene Gotti, John's brother, and his friend Angelo "Quack Quack" Ruggiero. The majority of the evidence came via Castellano's wiretapped conversations held in his kitchen.

Before the case would get to trial, Castellano had to deal with Ruggiero. Ruggiero, like Castellano, had no fear of talking freely over the phone. This time, his big mouth cost him big time. The feds had bugged Ruggiero's phone in 1980 and had recorded the chatty gangster criticizing and even ridiculing Castellano. Moreover, Ruggiero gave the feds ample stories about the family business, its drug deals, and his personal disdain for Big Paul.

One of the most damaging conversations was caught by FBI agents listening to a bug at a Brooklyn restaurant in 1983. In the conversation, Gerry Langella, the acting head of the Colombo crime family, and capo Dominic "Donny Shacks" Montemarano discussed Castellano's shortcomings and plans.

In Selwyn Raab's book, *Five Families: The Rise, Decline, and Resurgence of America's Most Powerful Mafia Empires*, Ruggiero claimed that Castellano had "denied his militants" any contact with Dellacroce.

"I think he's going to whack Neil," said Ruggiero. Montemarano and Langella opined that Castellano was also going to silence "Johnny," referring to Gotti. Ruggiero added: "(He) badmouths his own family."

Langella then described a recent meeting he'd had with Dellacroce: "I think I told Neil I know this cocksucker's (Castellano) badmouthing you. Let me tell you something, he ain't gonna get away with it no more, somebody's gonna . . ."

Such a dialogue was, in retrospect, hardly surprising, considering the animosity Ruggiero and others felt toward Big Paul. Still, Ruggiero had done the unthinkable, according to Mafia tradition: he'd denounced his don to a rival Mafia family. Such actions defied the Mob's longstanding rule of *omerta*.

Ironically, the family's divergent views on drugs and drug trafficking formed the foundation of Ruggiero's disdain for his boss. Although Castellano prohibited his subordinates from dealing drugs, he himself had powder on his fingers from his own covert drug jobs. Ruggiero believed Castellano was earning big bucks from the tributes offered by his capos, who themselves were selling heroin. Castellano also had a financial stake in supporting "the winning side" in the Bonanno family civil war in the early 1980s. Castellano, word had it, "was getting secret payments from the Bonannos' narcotics undertakings," according to Raab. Ultimately, Ruggiero said in wiretapped conversations, the Big Boss was a hypocrite when it came to dealing drugs.

As Castellano awaited trial, he learned about Ruggiero's dialogues with the Colombos and other wiretapped conversations. If the speculated content of the tapes was true, Ruggiero had broken Castellano's rules on drug trafficking. Castellano knew he had to get his hands on the tapes, especially after the material was given to Ruggiero's lawyers. Castellano believed that the drug indictments and the damaging conversations on the tapes would be ammo for him to bring down, or at least weaken, the Dellacroce clan—including John Gotti.

"By law, when a person is charged with a crime based on evidence gathered from a wiretap, he's given transcripts of the taped material to aid in his defense," said author Anthony Bruno, in an article for Tru Crime TV. "Ruggiero was presented with boxes of such transcripts, and it wasn't long before Big Paul sent down word that he wanted to see them. If his men were dealing dope, he wanted to know about it. Ruggiero told Castellano that he was innocent, that it was a bum rap, and that the feds had no case against him. (In fact, Ruggiero had borrowed $200,000 from Castellano for a drug deal, telling the boss that it was for a pornography enterprise.) Castellano, however, could not be placated. He insisted that he see the transcripts."

Ruggiero refused to give up the tapes, saying "there's some, some good friends of mine on those fuckin' tapes." He sought support from Dellacroce, who managed to hold off Castellano into 1985. But Castellano was getting desperate; he needed to know what was in those transcripts, and he was desperate to know which members of his family supported him, and which did not. As his trial approached, Castellano more than ever needed to know who "had his back," and who wanted to drive a blade into it. As the weeks and months passed, Dellacroce, who was now dying of cancer, was no longer an asset to Ruggiero. Ruggiero refused to give in to the will of Castellano, who he saw as the "white collar" shell of a boss of the Brooklyn faction. With Dellacroce helpless, Ruggiero turned to his childhood pal, John Gotti. By now, Gotti had more than his fill of Castellano's meddling in the ways of "the real wiseguys." Castellano, meanwhile, was ready to ice Gotti and Ruggiero if he didn't get his hands on the transcripts.

Gotti, despite his contempt for Castellano, also feared Big Paul. And he was miffed at Ruggiero's lack of discipline that had led to his conversations being recorded. He grabbed his friend by the collar, and according to Raab, rebuked him.

"Angelo, what does Cosa Nostra mean? Cosa Nostra means that the boss is your boss. You understand? Forget about all this nonsense."

In June 1985, Dellacroce warned both Gotti and Ruggiero that continued refusal to turn over the tapes would lead to a fracture between the two factions that could never be repaired. "I've been trying to make you get away with these tapes," he told Ruggiero. "But Jesus Christ almighty, I can't stop the guy from always bringin' it up

. . . Then you, then we know what we gotta do then, we go and roll it up and go to war. I don't know if that's what you want."

Ultimately, Castellano never received the tapes. The battle lines had been drawn between the two factions of the Gambino family. There was no turning back now, for Castellano or for Gotti.

The Mafia Commission Trial, as it became known, would run from February 25, 1985, through November 19, 1986, and severely undermine the power of the Commission, a panel consisting of key New York family Mob figures who acted as a pseudoboard of directors over local Mafia activities. Among those indicted were Castellano; Anthony "Fat Tony" Salerno, boss of the Genovese crime family; Carmine "Junior" Persico, head of the Colombo family; Anthony "Tony Ducks" Corallo, don of the Lucchese crime family; and Philip "Rusty" Rastelli, boss of the Bonanno family.

A *Time* magazine article dubbed the Mafia Commission Trial one of "the most significant assaults on the infrastructure of organized crime since the high command of the Chicago Mafia was swept away in 1943." The story also quoted Giuliani's plan for the Mob: "Our approach . . . is to wipe out the five families."

Castellano had been released on $3 million bail. But Giuliani was the least of Big Paul's problems. His growing number of nemeses feared that Castellano would break the Mob law of *omerta* and strike a deal with the feds. Couple the damaging wiretapped conversations with Castellano's age and fear of jail, and wiseguys such as Gotti had reason to doubt whether Castellano would keep his mouth shut.

Castellano's weakening grip on the Gambino family became yet more tenuous when on December 2, 1985, Dellacroce died of lung cancer. Punctuating his poor judgment of the modus operandi of his family, Castellano declined to attend Dellacroce's funeral, a disgraceful act for a man in his position and a critical error in judgment. With Dellacroce out of the way, wiseguys such as Gotti saw their opportunity to remove a man some considered an embarrassment to the Gambino name. Also, Gotti feared that without the protection of his ally, Dellacroce, Castellano would either demote him or kill him.

Castellano further alienated his rank and file when he appointed his bodyguard and loan shark, Tommy Bilotti, as the new underboss. Bilotti was recognized as a loyal family member, but those who opposed the appointment said Bilotti was too inexperienced and lacked the business finesse necessary to hold such a lofty position.

In many ways, Tommy Bilotti was the antithesis of Castellano; at the time of his promotion, Bilotti was forty-five, some twenty-five years junior to his boss. Unlike the proud, stately Castellano, Bilotti was a short, squat, hard-headed loan shark with little interest in personal and business propriety. He wore suits that often appeared selected at random from his closet, the pants often clashing with the shirts. A poorly fitting toupee threatened to fall off at any moment, and many of his detractors dubbed Bilotti "The Rug." He preferred brute force over conversation, violence over white collar crime. Where Castellano used words to negotiate with others, Bilotti wielded a Louisville Slugger to his enemies' heads to get his point across. Publicly, Bilotti was listed as the vice president of the Staten Island concrete company Scare-Mix, a Castellano family holding that specialized in sub-contracts on city and state projects. To Gotti, Bilotti was of no consequence.

Gotti began to gauge the loyalty of those in the pro-Castellano quarters. Had Dellacroce died a few years earlier, Gotti might have lacked the experience and wherewithal to plot the assassination of his boss. Now, however, he'd advanced beyond being a mere street punk whose primary weapons were his fists and a gun. Gotti had developed the leadership skills and the expertise to map out a strategy that would change the landscape of the Mafia world. Moreover, he "had the balls" to call the hit.

Now, if John Gotti, or a Gotti associate, spoke or asked questions, people listened. Salvatore "Sammy the Bull" Gravano listened. He'd grown weary with Castellano's greed with their rackets, while depriving the rank and file their just due. Gotti used Gravano to approach Frankie DeCicco about a hit on Castellano. Gotti knew that DeCicco, a capo in the family, was an old-school mobster who appreciated the way Dellacroce had conducted business. In speaking with DeCicco, Gravano learned that the capo, like Gravano, also disliked Castellano's alliance between the construction industry and the Genovese family, which stuffed Castellano's pockets with cash but left Castellano's soldiers empty-handed. Furthermore, both men resented Big Paul for permitting the Genovese clan to knock off a Gambino capo in Connecticut over a money dispute. Castellano was "selling out the family," Gravano told DeCicco, and the don had to be dealt with. DeCicco, possibly the last buffer between Castellano and the Dellacroce wing, was sold.

Still, there were a number of challenges remaining. To date, for a member of New York's Five Families to kill—or engineer the killing of—a Mob godfather required the express approval of the Commission, the governing board of New York's Five Families. Gotti knew it was fruitless to lobby the Commission for Castellano's elimination; Castellano had for years been considered the Boss of Bosses, and none of the other family heads would publicly okay the hit. By now, Gotti was accustomed to using subtlety to solve challenges rather than mere brute force. He dispatched associates to meet with important members of the other crime families—Lucchese, Colombo, and Bonanno—to gauge their feelings about a possible hit on Castellano. He avoided the Genovese family, whose ties to Castellano were too strong. The consensus: hit Big Paul.

Gotti and Gravano would oversee the assassination from a car parked across the street. Their plan was as embarrassing in its simplicity as Castellano's ignorance of his own impending peril. Gotti knew Castellano was a man who believed in negotiating and in "saving face." Doubtless Big Paul knew that spurning Dellacroce's funeral was a tactical miscue of epic proportions. They invited him to his favorite restaurant, Sparks Steak House, where Castellano would "pay his respects" to Dellacroce's son, Buddy. A Mob leader in touch with the pulse of his family would have suspected an act of treachery. But Castellano was merely focused on making amends with the Dellacroce clan.

In his article for the Tru Crime TV program *Gangsters & Outlaws: Bosses, The Last Mafia Icon*, author Allan May wrote that final arrangements for the meeting took place the day before the scheduled hit.

> Eleven conspirators met at Gravano's office on Stillwell Avenue. According to Gravano, the four designated shooters were Vincent Artuso, John Carneglia, and Eddie Lino and his brother-in-law Salvatore Scala. The designated back-up shooter, Anthony "Tony Roach" Rampino, would be standing across the street from Sparks Steak House, while Angelo Ruggiero, Joseph Watts and Iggy Alogna would be stationed at 46th Street and Second Avenue to facilitate the escape. Frank DeCicco would be inside the restaurant where a meeting was to take place. He would be joined there by capos James Failla and Daniel Marino, who were not part of the plot.
>
> "The more we thought about it, the better it looked," Sammy said. "We concluded that nine days before Christmas, around five to six o'clock at night, in the middle of Manhattan, in the middle of rush hour, in the middle of the crush of all them shoppers buying presents, there would be literally thousands of people on the street, hurrying this way and that. The hit would only take a few seconds, and the confusion would be in our favor. Nobody would be expecting anything like this, least of all Paul. And being able to disappear afterwards in the crowds would be in our favor. So we decide this is when and where it's going to happen."

According to Gravano, the hit team did not know of their exact assignment and the identity of the targets until the afternoon of the shooting. Gathered in a park on Manhattan's Lower East Side, the foursome discussed the logistics of the shooting. Wrote May:

> The four shooters were dressed alike—long light colored trench coats and black fur Russian, or Cossack, style hats. The reasoning for this was to draw attention to the outfits, not the men wearing them. Gravano told the FBI that he and Gotti arrived near Sparks

Steak House close to five o'clock in a Lincoln driven by John. Famed New York Police Detective Joseph Coffey, in an interview with Court TV's Rikki Klieman years later, doubted the two were in the vicinity of the restaurant. Gravano claimed that after circling the block, they parked where from their vantage point they would have a clear view of the front of the restaurant. Moments later Bilotti in a black Lincoln pulled alongside Gotti's car and waited for the light to change. Using a walkie-talkie Gravano notified the others that Castellano was proceeding through the intersection.

Bilotti parked the Lincoln in an illegal parking zone; a Patrolmen's Benevolent Association sign posted on the dashboard beneath the windshield allowed him to do so. He stepped from the Lincoln. Castellano emerged from the car just as the hit men stepped forward.

Five shots (there are conflicting reports of six shots being fired) slammed into the don's head and torso; Big Paul slumped to the pavement, the twisted corpse of what had been the Boss of Bosses.

At the sound of gunfire, the unarmed Bilotti peered through the driver's window. He saw Big Paul battered with bullets and blood streaming from his head. Bilotti hardly expected what followed. Assassins turned their guns on the driver-turned-underboss.

One shooter's gun jammed; another hit man stepped in and fired repeatedly at Bilotti. John Carneglia, who'd just blasted Castellano, walked around the car and fired a round into Bilotti's lifeless frame. Biolotti's bullet-riddled body lay in the street as passersby sped from the scene. The assassins, meanwhile, strode off calmly into the crowd and disappeared up Second Avenue, where getaway cars awaited them.

Meanwhile, Gotti and Gravano cruised past the restaurant as calmly as if they themselves were about to dine. According May, Gravano looked down at Castellano's body and said simply, "He's gone."

Back inside Sparks, DeCicco, Failla and Marino also heard the gunfire and raced from the restaurant. They walked down 46th Street, where they encountered Thomas Gambino, Castellano's nephew. He was en route to the Sparks meeting. May described their meeting:

> "Your uncle's been shot," said DeCicco.
> "Is he dead?" Gambino asked.
> "He is, Tommy," DeCicco confirmed.
> "Jesus, what's going on?" Gambino inquired.
> "Don't worry, everyone else is okay. Get to your car and leave. We'll be in touch," DeCicco assured.

The following day, newspapers trumpeted Castellano's demise. "Reputed Mobster Leader is Slain," rang the Associated Press's headline. "Paul Castellano was, until two hours ago, the head of the largest organized crime family in the United States," said Thomas Sheer, an FBI organized crime specialist, in the AP's article. "It could be the beginning of a crime war. But only time will tell that. This undoubtedly will trigger some sort of reaction. It's part of the changing of the (Mafia) guard that's been going on for the last twenty-five years."

The FBI did not need the killers' descriptions to theorize who okayed the job. The hours of recorded dialogue they'd collected from bugs in Castellano's home assured them that the man in charge of the assassination was John Gotti. Still, investigators were unable to find a single shred of tangible evidence against Gotti. With the swift elimination of Paul Castellano, John Gotti not only had preserved his safety, he'd catapulted himself to the top of the Gambino family hierarchy.

The changing of the guard didn't precipitate the massive war between the New York families that Sheer had predicted. Although it was considered taboo for a don to be assassinated without the approval of the New York Commission, few wiseguys raised their voices in protest. John Gotti had already sown the seeds of his appointment to the head of the Gambino family. His final hurdle was convincing Gambino family consigliere Joe N. Gallo. Devoid of family muscle to support him in his own bid to become boss, the seventy-five-year-old Castellano ally counted his losses and his blessings, and helped install Gotti as new boss of the Gambino family.

Several days after the double murder, Gallo organized a meeting with the majority of the family's capos. The conference, in which Gotti would be sworn in as the new don, was held after hours at Caesar's East, a few blocks from Sparks. Gravano, ironically, was a part-owner of the restaurant. During the meeting, Gallo announced that an internal investigation would be undertaken to find and punish Castellano's murderers. Such talk was mere posturing, of course, since everyone in the room knew Gotti had masterminded the assassination. Still, Gallo's pronouncement helped to put closure on the killing and "absolve" Gotti of any part in the double hit. Because of the *omerta*, Gallo and Gotti knew no wiseguys would ever blow the whistle on Gotti. Gallo also went out of his way to assure the other four families that the Gambino enclave was "intact, strong, and united"—a subtle message to the other families to watch their step.

At age forty-six, John Gotti was the new godfather of the powerful Gambino crime family.

The fallout from the Castellano family also thwarted the prosecution's case in the Commission Trial; it nullified as evidence much of the taped conversations, because select information pertained exclusively to Castellano. The case would go to trial, but without "direct Gambino family involvement in the case," according to Raab.

In a sad yet ironic epilogue, Castellano was denied the respect due him, perhaps due any Catholic, when the Roman Catholic Archdiocese announced that it would prohibit a public Mass for the slain Mobster "because of his notoriety and background."

CHAPTER 7

Preppy and Practically Perfect ... Except He's a Killer

At first glance, the scene being acted out on the television screen is reminiscent of a harmless college fraternity or sorority party, perhaps a case of an intoxicated frat brother titillating a few wide-eyed coeds.

Except that this fun-loving prank was recorded, and now the home movie runs in its entirety on the electronic magazine program *A Current Affair*. The date is May 16, 1988, and millions of viewers watch the shenanigans of a stunningly handsome twenty-one-year-old man and a quartet of ogling pajama-clad female friends. The center of attention in this video romp is Robert Chambers Jr. Of note among the viewers is Ellen Levin.

As the video progresses, Chambers's mood and actions slowly turn from playful to frightening. He and the four women take turns dancing and teasing each other; they chat, they laugh—and then the dark side of Chambers emerges. In one scene, he raises his hands to his neck and pretends to choke himself. Then Chambers picks up a child's doll. Beaming into the camera, he gleefully twists the doll's head around.

"Oops, I think I killed her," he jokes. "Both eyes are . . ."

Chambers stops in mid-sentence, as one of the women kicks him and urges him to stop his bizarre behavior. Chambers does, but by the conclusion of the thirty-minute "secret home video," America has gotten to know the evil side of Robert Chambers. It is a haunting, dark shadow of evil cast from a squeaky-clean persona. For weeks, Ellen Levin intuitively knew that Chambers possessed a dark side, even when others didn't. Her daughter, Jennifer, knew Chambers well; she had befriended him, dated him, liked him, and perhaps even loved him. She'd seen Chambers's unseemly side, his need for acceptance, for drugs, for the high life. She saw how he could cloak his rage in playfulness. She witnessed it up until the moment Robert killed her. She was just eighteen years old.

Some five months after an unidentified source recorded Chamber's eerie slumber party video, and a mere few days before *A Current Affair* aired this same clip, Chambers admitted to unintentionally killing Levin, his former girlfriend and a popular member of New York's elite Upper East Side society. Levin's body was discovered in a grove of trees in Central Park. Her bra had been pushed above her breasts and her skirt shoved to her waist. She lay spread eagle on the ground. Investigators at the scene identified marks on her neck and body.

The news stunned both the Levin and Chambers families, and their circle of friends and associates. How could two young adults who both came from a wealthy part of the city, who enjoyed so many privileges and were envied and admired by so many of their peers, end up in Central Park—the starlet dead and her name to be sullied by the media, the star with his life shattered, looking at a future behind prison bars?

As is often the case in incongruously senseless capital crimes of this nature, there was more to the story of the Preppy Murder and the lives of the people involved than meets the eye. Both were affected deeply by familial and environmental influences. Ostensibly living privileged lives among the East Side's elite, Chambers and Levin, in retrospect, were drawn together by what they lacked. Levin wanted to party and commiserate with Manhattan's "A crowd"; Chambers had a deep-seated need for love and acceptance, especially from his mother and girls.

To understand why and how Robert Chambers killed Jennifer Levin, you must travel back in time, to Ireland, long before Robert Chambers Jr. and Jennifer Levin were born.

Phyllis Chambers was the dominant figure in her son Robert's life. Born in Ireland and raised on a farm with her five siblings, Phyllis dreamed of the day she could escape her bleak existence. She took her first step toward a better life by studying nursing in Dublin. Afterward, she availed herself of the first-hand training available in local hospitals, delivering babies for the less fortunate. She also cared for those who suffered from tuberculosis or other communicable diseases.

She learned from this experience two important things: how to nurture and care for others, especially those in need, and that she desperately wanted to escape from this low social status. She yearned for the best in life—socially, intellectually, financially, and emotionally. Like many others desperate to escape their wretched existences in Europe, she came to the United States seeking to make her dreams come true.

Phyllis quickly and easily got a nursing job at a New York hospital; she also took on private assignments, some of which connected her with New York's elite and wealthy. One assignment vastly affected her thinking and dreams and future: she cared for John "John-John" F. Kennedy Jr., son of President John F. Kennedy. It was a life and lifestyle Phyllis gladly entered and sought to emulate.

While Phyllis's client base and career expanded, so did her love life. She met a young man named Robert (Bob) Chambers, a man of substance, with strong pedigree and an amicable nature. Bob Chambers came from an Irish-English family that had been in America for generations. Bob and his family wanted for little; they owned a house in Westchester and a cabin on lovely Lake Placid. Bob led a comfortable life; he had attended top private schools and then attended Mitchell College in Connecticut and American University in Washington, D.C. In 1965 Phyllis and Bob Chambers married; a year later their son, Robert Emmet Chambers Jr., was born. He was angelic-looking, with stunning deep blue eyes and pearl-white skin. This look—gorgeous and gentle and innocent— would be his physical hallmark and would create an indelible image in millions of people's minds.

Phyllis Chambers, not surprisingly, fell in love with her son, and on him she imposed her dreams of greatness. She enrolled him first in the prestigious Manhattan nursery, St. David's School, just off Fifth Avenue. Unlike the strict Irish schools in which Phyllis was raised, St. David's was a lenient and nurturing environment. On some level, their academic philosophy and Phyllis's child-rearing philosophy diverged. Phyllis was a strict but loving mother who demanded propriety and manners from her young son: yes, sir; no, ma'am; thank you—be polite. Fit in with the A-list crowd.

Unfortunately for Phyllis and her son, Bob Chambers was not fitting into any elite crowd. Bob had enjoyed his drinks, as far back as his teen years. But now he was drinking too much, Phyllis decided. Sometimes he didn't come home; other times he was not where he said he would be. It is uncertain whether Bob Chambers became a victim of liquor because he could not live up to his wife's standards; certainly, as time would prove, he was not comfortable in her expanding elite social circles. And Bob Chambers also struggled to make an impact on his son's world.

Despite the family discord, Phyllis remained steadfast in her desire to provide her son with the best the world could offer. In 1974, she enrolled him in the prestigious Knickerbocker Greys, an after-school group that taught well-to-do boys discipline and patriotism through military drills. Its moniker, "The Social Register's Private Little Army," underscored its vaunted standing on the East Side of New York.

The Greys provided another portal into society's privileged world; its alums included young men with surnames such as Vanderbilt, Rockefeller, and Lindsay. Phyllis spun wild fantasies of the name Chambers being mentioned in the same breath as these other well-regarded names.

Robert, now age eight, held no such delusions of grandeur; he simply enjoyed the marching and the military drills. He was proud to wear the revered Greys uniform, and he dreamed of one day wielding the sword awarded to those who made sergeant's rank. Best yet, Robert Chambers Jr. enjoyed giving orders; it was better than taking them. Robert became a superior cadet. He drilled well and with precision, worked gladly in Greys' functions, and handled with skill the sword and rifle.

As Robert rose in stature and rank in the organization, so did his family. Phyllis moved the family to a comparatively modest apartment on Park Avenue, not far from Armory. Phyllis continued to work long hours as a nurse, but she found the time to pursue her passion—organizational and charity work. Phyllis began raising money for St. David's, and she joined the prestigious Altar Society of the Church of St. Thomas More.

Like his mother, Robert Jr. quickly found himself on a unique life path. By age 10, he was thriving at St. David's, making friends and trying to fit in. He remained the polite, well-mannered boy Phyllis expected and had raised. But as Robert became more and more popular, he began to change—at first, only out of his mother's gaze.

One time, a friend at St. David's thought he saw Robert or one of his close friends stealing money from his bank during the friend's birthday party. Another boy, from a different private school, bribed a man to purchase alcohol from a neighborhood package store—a liquor shop recommended by Robert Chambers Jr. The rumors spread and multiplied over the succeeding weeks and months: Chambers was now drinking booze and smoking marijuana.

Notwithstanding these vices, Chambers was growing into a man, and a whole lot faster than other boys in his group. By age twelve, he was taller than most boys his age, and all the drilling with the Greys had chiseled his body. His face was beginning to show the boyish handsomeness that would make girls' eyes roll wistfully. Robert became an altar boy at St. David's and earned a number of medals for marksmanship with the Greys. He was elected to the Greys' elite Honor Guard. He was the proverbial apple of his mother's eye. Phyllis followed suit and advanced her own career by joining the board of directors for the Greys; in 1979, she was named the group's president.

She then enrolled her son in The Browning School, another prestigious prep school located on the East Side of Manhattan. Robert quickly adapted to the jet-set lifestyle of New York's A-list crowd: fast cars, fast parties, fast drugs, and fast sex. Chambers's stunning good looks and shy charm drew girls to him in droves. And these cliques of friends hung out at New York City's elite clubs, including Studio 54.

It was a great life, but it presented challenges for Chambers. While his friends may have come from wealthy families, Robert did not. The partying cost money, the drugs cost more, and Robert had basically one way to raise cash to maintain his jet-setting lifestyle. Before long, the neighbors and even Chambers's friends began to whisper again—is Robert stealing? Speculation grew during the school year when Browning was beset by a rash of vandalism and a number of robberies. The school's headmaster was worried; he didn't suspect Robert, but he also did not approve of the social circles Robert frequented.

That band of friends continued to expand, and Robert Chambers continued to be the center of attraction, even if he did not seek to be.

During one school year, he and some school friends traveled to Vermont to enjoy a few days of skiing at Gore Mountain. Also on the trip was a fourteen-year-old coed named Leilia Van Baker, a girl Robert had befriended a few years earlier. At that time, neither could foresee the tragic consequences of their friendship. One night, Chambers and a few friends began partying—Robert had brought enough beer and whiskey to intoxicate the group for much of the trip. In fact, one girl drank so much that she suffered alcohol poisoning and was hospitalized.

Robert Chambers may have seen the trip as nothing more than harmless partying; the administration at Browning did not. And when Robert was found to be in possession of a Browning teacher's credit cards, the administration had no choice but to expel him.

For most students, expulsion from two prestigious preparatory schools would mark the end of their academic careers. But Robert Chambers was no ordinary student. Despite his growing problems, he still boasted solid references from St. David's and the Knickerbocker Greys; he still carried himself with the usual well-mannered charm that bewitched even the most perspicacious person. And in his mother, he had a top-notch PR executive.

Seeking to stop her son's downward spiral, Phyllis rushed Robert to a chemical dependency facility in Louisiana. She was confident he'd come back clean and refreshed, and walk a straight line to Harvard or Oxford or Duke. One day, he'd be a CEO at a major company, she believed.

After her son was expelled from the prestigious Choate-Rosemary Hall in Wallingford, Connecticut, Phyllis utilized her hard work and a glowing recommendation from St. David's to gain him acceptance into York Prep, a coed school on New York's Upper East Side. It was February 1982, and Robert's future appeared bright. By age sixteen, Robert Chambers had grown into the man all the girls wanted and the icon the boys wanted to become. Chambers, ironically, accepted the attention with little fanfare; he hardly sought the spotlight. He did, however, seek the quick fix only booze and drugs could bring. His two years at York were merely a continuation of a personal battle that had begun in his preteen years.

Phyllis continued to downplay her son's problems, but perhaps for the first time, Bob Chambers began to see the dark and dangerous side of his son. Now clean and sober, Bob Chambers also began to question his wife's laissez-faire handling of her son. The Chambers family was slowly beginning to fall apart.

On New Years' Eve 1982, the Chambers's apartment was burglarized; among the many items stolen were Phyllis's clothes, jewelry, a camera, and many other cherished family items. The neighbors, many of whom already considered Robert a thief, immediately suspected him of committing the crime.

As the winter ski season began to wane, Chambers sold a pair of stolen skis to a former York student he'd known named Brock Pernice. Chambers had wanted $200 for the pair of "old family skis." Pernice had only $100. Chambers accepted it—at first. Days later Chambers visited Pernice, accompanied by two young men Pernice did not recognize. Chambers demanded the balance of the $200. When Pernice said he did not have the money, Chambers's thugs escorted the frightened Pernice to the bank. They suspiciously studied Pernice as he withdrew the money.

Robert's downward spiral continued—more partying, less study, more accusations of stealing (some confirmed) and selling hot goods. Finally, on the day of his graduation from York Prep, Robert Chambers received only an empty diploma case. He was stunned.

Ironically, Robert's bad boy image merely made him more admirable. In fact, behind the scenes, Robert's old friend Leilia Van Baker was promoting Robert to another friend. The girl's name was Jennifer Levin; like Chambers, Levin enjoyed the party scene and hanging with the in crowd. Maybe they could meet one day, Baker suggested.

Robert Chambers Jr. had other intentions, at least for now. He finished his high school education and then enrolled at Boston University. The results were predictable: more booze, coke, and goofing off.

By December 1984, Robert was out of BU, accused of stealing a roommate's credit card. Perhaps for the first time in their relationship, Phyllis accepted the painful reality that Robert's problems were serious. She kicked her son out of their home and told him to get a job.

Robert did. He got more than one job, in fact. He also enrolled at Hunter College, but nothing changed. By 1985, he was free-basing cocaine and committing more burglaries to support his expensive habits. He even bragged to friends about some of these exploits. Others believed he was stealing money from them.

In 1986, Robert grew tired of Hunter College. Now he and his pals were hanging out at local bars such as Dorrian's Red Hand, and Robert was captivating his friends with wild dreams of attending Harvard or starting a business of his own. That was the dream. In reality, he stole traveler's checks from a tourist; he also burgled a credit card from a girlfriend's mother and then went off on a wild spending spree, purchasing just the right clothes to fit in with the elite crowd.

And then a strange thing happened: A shoe store clerk alerted the owner of the stolen card Robert possessed. The woman knew of Robert's penchant for lifting items, and she planned to call Phyllis about the incident. And she planned to press charges.

Phyllis was stunned. Couldn't they work something out? Sympathizing with the plight of the Chambers parents, the woman agreed to drop charges if Robert got treatment for his drug dependency. The next day, Robert left for the Hazelden Clinic in Minnesota. After completing the program, he returned home to New York and convinced his mother to allow him to live with her, instead of in a halfway house, as was suggested. He'd cleaned up his act, had big dreams, and maybe would attend Columbia.

But the dreams were empty and so were Robert's promises. Soon, he was back to the booze, the partying, and the wasted hours. Robert's fate awaited him, as did Levin, whom Robert described as "the best-looking girl in the world."

Like Robert Chambers Jr., Jennifer Levin enjoyed and needed the acceptance of others, was drawn to the spotlight, and desperately fought to find equanimity in her incomplete family life. While popularity came to Robert, Levin struggled to be in society's in crowd.

Three years younger than her sister Danielle, Jennifer Levin may not have been the prettier of the two Levin girls, but she was the craftier. Bubbly and filled with creative energy, she used her effervescence, charm, and passion for fashion to connect with others. Growing up in Long Island, she emulated her father Steve and his father, both of whom longed to be actors. She dressed up in sequins and ribbons, wore her mother Ellen's high heels and makeup, and paraded around as if she were on Broadway. As a child, she wanted, more than anything else, to fit into her older sister Danielle's crowd.

As time passed, Jennifer learned that making others laugh would help her through the many changes and challenges she would encounter in her life.

The first change came at home. Both her parents could be emotional and mercurial, and their differing interests and goals eventually drove a wedge in their marriage. Steve was the pragmatist, focused on facts and figures in his real estate business. Ellen was the idealist with a bent for the arts. When Jennifer was five, the Levins separated and later divorced. Ellen remained in Long Island with the girls, and Steve moved to Manhattan.

The breakup not only affected the girls but also Ellen, who sought a change from the cookie-cutter world of Long Island and its lifestyle of two kids, two cars, and tailored lawns. About a year later, Ellen and the girls moved to California, where they rented an apartment that was rumored to have belonged to actor Rudolph Valentino. Hollywood, with all its drama and pomp and circumstance, was the perfect stage for a blossoming six-year-old who adored the spotlight.

In her book, *Wasted: The Preppie Murder*, Linda Wolfe underscores the lengths to which Jennifer would go to gain attention:

> One day, she paraded down Hollywood Boulevard in a big hat and her mother's high heels. Another day, visiting a restaurant owned by a friend of her mother's, she played waitress, clearing tables and,

not yet comprehending the principles of tipping, amusingly telling guests she hoped they'd return soon while at the same time handing them quarters.

But life would not remain a Hollywood movie. Steve Levin had fallen in love with a young widow named Arlene Voorhust. Jennifer, who had an eye for beauty, considered Arlene gorgeous. But like most eight-year-old children introduced to a rival for their attention, Jennifer resented Arlene. When Jennifer was eight, Steve and Arlene married. Neither of the girls attended the wedding, for reasons unclear today.

By 1979, Ellen Levin had tired of the Hollywood lifestyle and all that went with it. She moved the girls back east to Manorhaven, an enclave of Port Washington, New York, and enrolled Jennifer in the local school. Now eleven, Jennifer was in the midst of the prepubescent awkward stage; all arms and legs, with crooked teeth, big ears, and lifeless straight hair. At first, Jennifer hated being the new girl in the school, but her sense of alienation was short-lived. As she had done time and again, Jennifer relied on her infectious personality to win over others. Before long, Jennifer was enjoying sleepovers and parties galore. The following year, she attended John Philip Sousa, one of two junior high schools in Port Washington. Jennifer initially was upset; most of her friends from sixth grade were attending the other school. But once again, it took little time for Jennifer to make friends. Before long, she was at the hub of the school's "A crowd."

But the following year, Jennifer struggled socially and academically. She no longer was the darling of the elite clique, and her grades—especially in reading—were subpar. Jen wasn't exactly worried about the grades; she was, however, concerned about the stories students had been spreading about her. She wanted to transfer to the other school, Weber Middle School. In early 1982, Ellen Levin bought a larger house in the Weber School District. The white stucco two-story building with an attic on top had shingles that were chipped and cracked. The yard was small. Hollywood it was not. Still, Jennifer adapted. She hung out with a covey of junior high school girls and a handful of older high school boys. She continued to entertain friends with her comedic antics; perhaps that was in part because of her physical self-image. As she entered her teens, Jennifer considered herself too gawky, her skin inconsistent and blemished, and her breasts too prominent. The boys, however, disagreed, and Jennifer enjoyed dates with a few of the best-looking guys in the school. But when you're in junior high, guys and girls mostly enjoy just hanging out; such was the case in Jennifer's circles. They spent lunchtime in a secluded stairwell beside a nearby church. Occasionally, the group skipped class and spent the time at a friend's home, smoking marijuana. Eventually, Jennifer gave pot a try.

After struggling through her final year at Weber, Jennifer moved out of her mother's home in Port Washington and in with her father and stepmother, now living in trendy, upscale SoHo. Jennifer sought the stability and guidance her father would give. Stability included a new school, one where Jennifer could keep up with her classmates. They chose Baldwin, a West Side private school that helped students with learning disabilities. Steve hoped his daughter would get the academic support she needed.

Now fourteen, Jennifer quickly adapted to the trendy scene of Baldwin. She cut her hair in a punk style and donned hipper clothes that showed off her now mature figure. Not surprisingly, she quickly developed many new friends, just as easily as she always had. Sometimes the group hung out at Central Park after school. During that first semester, Jennifer met a young man named Brock Pernice, and the pair quickly began dating regularly. Like Jennifer, Pernice was full of life; he was the grandson of Broadway producer Alexander Cohen and was a student at York School. It was the same Brock Pernice who'd bought the "used" skis from old friend Robert Chambers.

That fall, Jennifer and her friends began hanging around the revamped Studio 54. Once a haven for drugs and disco, the club's original owners were serving prison terms for tax fraud. Now, the club accepted fourteen-year-olds, *if* they fit into the elite crowd.

Jennifer Levin and many of her friends weren't A-crowd caliber, but they still were among the Studio's "B" list. That meant dressing for the occasion—fancy clothes, stylish shoes, lots of makeup to stand out. Steve Levin wasn't so sure, and he kept close tabs on his daughter. She could not go out on weeknights. When she did get together with friends, she had to call him regularly and keep him abreast of her activities and her location. Still, one night, Jennifer got so drunk at Studio that her father grounded her.

Time was speeding along, and Jennifer, like many girls approaching their sixteenth birthday, had two things on her mind: boys and parties. Especially boys, for Jennifer held the notion of losing her virginity and falling in love. She and her friends often traversed the city and Greenwich Village scoping out guys. Jennifer began writing poetry, often with love as the theme. Once the four-year-old who dazzled others with her charm and effervescence, she now sought to become the girl no young man could turn down.

When she found the right boy with whom she did enter into womanhood, she felt triumphant. Just a few days later, however, Jennifer felt her heart sink when she saw the same boy hugging another girl at a party. She returned to Pernice.

In 1984, while living and working in Long Island, Jennifer met a girl who would forever change her life. The girl was Leilia Van Baker, a pretty blond who was at the hub of New York's elite crowd. She had been a regular at the discos and promised to introduce Jennifer to the most handsome and exciting guys around. At the top of the list was the best-looking of all, Robert Chambers. Jennifer began to attend private parties at Studio 54.

By early 1985, the party scene had begun to switch to the smaller, more intimate bars. Eventually, Pernice took Jennifer to Dorrian's Red Hand, an unpretentious bar with a fireplace and an old-fashioned wooden bar, complete with interesting figurines and other bric-a-brac. Dorrian's soon became their favorite night spot.

During her senior year, Jennifer's interest in drugs expanded; she also enjoyed intimate relations with a variety of young men. Her grades began to slip, her relationship with her father and stepmother began to deteriorate, and she still considered her mother irresponsible and too doting.

She needed someone. So did Robert Chambers.

"I remember when I met her, she was Little Miss Innocent," former boyfriend Brock Pernice told *New York* magazine. "I saw her change, grow up real quick in the city. She wanted to be everyone's friend, and she put herself on their level. She would sound like different people with different friends. She even began to look like them." Eventually, fate took over. As the school year wound down, Robert Chambers was already dating a girl steadily. But in early summer of 1986, Robert spotted Levin at Dorrian's, partying with a friend.

For one of the few times in his life, Chambers was almost speechless. Levin, similarly, was stunned by Chambers's good looks and power over guys and girls alike. At six-foot-four and more than two hundred pounds, Chambers stood like a man among boys in the bar, revered by the doting women and admired by the merely human guys. He was, to Levin, almost overwhelmingly magnetic.

Later that night, the two popular stars spoke for the first time outside the bar. Robert attempted to retain his casual trademark cool and charm, while Levin, according to a friend, "turned a different color" in his presence. They did nothing but talk that night. In the second week of July, they spent the night together at his house. But Levin later told friends that Robert remained respectful of her and spent much of their time together lavishing her with compliments.

Still, even with sparks igniting between the two, Robert Chambers and Jennifer Levin enjoyed little more than a harmless summer fling. Robert continued seeing his girlfriend and, after a enjoying a brief vacation in California, Levin returned to the Hamptons for the remainder of August. She and Pernice also rekindled their stalled romance.

Levin seemed to have it all—popularity, her choice of young men, friends galore, and a stimulating party scene. She looked forward to attending college.

Meanwhile, Robert Chambers, according to friends, was a whirling dervish, desperate to reinvent himself and escape from a world that now seemed boring and false to him. But he'd played so many social games, told so many lies, stolen articles and stolen hearts, tried to live up to his mother's vaunted expectations . . . he'd lost track of himself. He sought counsel from his parish priest, and even made a second appointment to see him. But Robert Chambers Jr. never made it to the follow-up visit. That night, August 26, 1985, he was at Dorrian's, seated at the bar, sipping a shot of gloom. His friends wondered when he would snap. His girlfriend was with him, yet not with him.

On that fateful night, Robert Chambers Jr. was in his own world. Some friends later said that Robert was lamenting the death of a friend he'd met at rehab. Certainly, he had enough life challenges to kindle such chagrin. Whatever the specific reason, Robert was aloof and not even communicating with his girlfriend. Finally, the silence ended in an ugly explosion of emotions when she confronted Robert about his reticence.

The scene was now set for the final act in the Chambers–Levin drama. Unlike the morose Robert, Jennifer Levin was bouncy, ebullient, and in love with life when she and her friends entered the bar. She was, as Robert Chambers had previously noted, the belle of the ball—eyes wide and searching, her bright pretty face open and inviting.

"She was very flirtatious, definitely outgoing," said one unidentified young man in the *New York* magazine article. "You could tell by the way she flashed her eyes. She kissed me when we were introduced, and she didn't even know me."

Although she and Pernice were still romantically involved, Levin that night told her friends she wanted to grab Chambers and go home with him. Little did Jennifer Levin know that she was the spark to ignite Robert's fuse. During the evening, the moody Chambers virtually ignored his girlfriend. Finally, the pair exploded in an emotional scene, with her storming away. That opened the door for Levin to enter. By the early morning hours, the two were engaged in conversation. Their quiet talking continued until around 4:30 A.M., when she waved good-bye to her friends and left with Chambers. The two headed for Central Park, a spot both enjoyed but usually went to in groups.

Only Chambers knows exactly what followed, and he would later render his testimony on tape. However, according to published reports and other sources, an Upper East Side doctor jogged past the pair at around 5 A.M. Were they having sex? he wondered. Some twenty minutes later this same jogger passed Chambers and Levin once again, and this time thought he heard someone crying in distress. He asked if the pair was alright, and someone responded in the affirmative. The jogger went on his way, passing another runner moments later.

At about 6:15, a cyclist found Levin's body near Fifth Avenue and 83rd Street, behind the Metropolitan Museum of Art.

To the Central Park Precinct officers who arrived first on the scene, the crime had all the earmarks of a rape or sexual assault. The bruises around Levin's neck suggested she had been strangled. The bruises and bite marks on her torso all indicated she had lost a battle for her life. Local police officers called in detectives, and soon the crime scene was busy with investigators, forensics experts, and photographers. As police arrived at the crime scene, Robert Chambers stood by a stone wall of the museum watching quietly, numbly. He was in shock, friends later claimed, and not aware that Levin was dead. He did not call police. At some point, he returned home and caught a few hours of sleep.

Meanwhile, the NYPD's Crime Scene Unit (CSU) found on the body a wallet containing a torn dollar bill, fake identification cards, and a credit card that identified the dead girl as Jennifer Dawn Levin. Shortly afterwards, the Central Park Precinct took over the case, led by detective Michael McEntee, for whom this was his first case. McEntee found a pair of white panties some fifty feet away from the body. Also collected were jewelry and several pictures and a card for the Palladium nightclub that belonged to a friend of Levin. Police then interviewed a doorman at the Palladium who identified Levin from snapshots of her body. The investigation then led police to Steve Levin's Manhattan office; there, detectives disclosed Jennifer's death. Finally, they followed leads to Dorrian's and to witnesses who would eventually lead them to one person: Robert Chambers.

Elsewhere, Assistant Medical Examiner Maria Luz Alandy studied the body and determined that Levin had died of "asphyxia by strangulation." Police officials attributed the bruises on her neck to the strangulation and her own fingernails as she fought off her assailant.

But that was not the case, according to Chambers. When NYPD detectives called Chambers at home, he claimed Levin was with Pernice, on the other side of town. Pernice, however, was in Long Island at the time of the murder. Storytelling was for Robert Chambers as easy as stealing, snorting coke, or sipping whiskey. And it did not take long for him to concoct accounts of his whereabouts and actions on the night of the murder.

Unconvinced by Chambers's alibi, police visited the family's home on the afternoon following the murder. Chambers greeted them wearing sneakers, sweatpants, and a T-Shirt. His face was tattered with scratches. Where did you get the scratches? investigators asked. From the cat, said Chambers. He'd been playing with the animal—tossing it up in the air, actually—and the cat had sunk its claws into him. Later examination would reveal scratches across Chambers's chest and a minor injury to his right hand. What about the gouge on his right hand? From sanding a neighbor's floor with a psychotic sander, said Chambers without blinking.

This kid is smooth, the police officers thought. Too smooth, and the scratches don't add up. Neither does the kid's story. Sensing Chambers just might be Levin's assailant, police asked Robert to come back the Central Park Precinct house to help them investigate Levin's disappearance. No problem, said Chambers; he was happy to help find the "missing girl."

For nearly eight hours, a team of detectives interrogated Chambers, who spoke without an attorney. At first, Chambers denied even leaving Dorrian's with Levin. But as time passed, the investigators' interrogation methods began to poke holes in Chambers's story. Finally, at around 10 P.M., Chambers admitted responsibility for Levin's death, but claimed it was an accident. Levin was one of those horny chicks who liked rough sex, he said. They'd had sex three other times, after all. The previous night, her aggressiveness had cost her life.

From the interview emerged Chambers's taped account—the only account that exists—of the murder of Jennifer Levin.

Chambers and Levin walked to the park at around 4:50 A.M. and proceeded to a grassy area near the museum. Chambers said she became livid when he told her that the next time they would meet would be at Dorrian's. Perhaps he did not want to see her anymore. They argued. She still wanted to date him, she screamed. She scratched his face. Chambers dodged her advances; what could he do, after all—hit her with a stick? He got up to leave, but Levin encouraged him to stay. She wanted to talk, work things out. But first, she had to relieve herself. Chambers then said Levin disappeared momentarily to urinate by a tree.

Chambers said he recalled her returning from the bushes and tying his hands behind his back with her panties. How had a girl half his size done so? police asked. Chambers said he was leaning back, resting, and she surprised him. Then Levin knocked him to the ground, Chambers said. At first, he figured she was just goofing around. But then things got more serious; she "straddled him, facing away." Levin next stripped Chambers of his shirt and pants. She began to masturbate him.

Chambers claimed that he quickly grew tired of this routine and asked Levin to stop. She did not, he said, and instead squeezed his testicles firmly. She was hurting him. Chambers responded to the pain in his groin, he said, by freeing his hands; he reached up with his left arm. He pulled backward, on her neck, with all his strength. Eventually, she flipped her over his shoulder. She slammed into the ground. Chambers rose, put on his pants, turned to her and said, "Jennifer, come on, let's go." She did not respond. She did not move.

Yes, he had hurt her, Chambers admitted. But he had not meant to kill her; he was just protecting himself from a sexy, rough-playing girl who was for all intents and purposes raping him.

Assistant District Attorney Steve Saracco, one of many investigators to interview Chambers that night, refused to buy Chambers's version of the night in question. "I've been in this business for a while, and you're the first man I've seen raped in Central Park." Police also found it ridiculous that a six-foot-four, two hundred-pound man would be sexually assaulted and held at bay by a demure five-foot-four girl. After interviewing Chambers, they booked him on suspicion of murder. Reporter Mark Gado said in his report on TruTV Crime Library that before being booked, Chambers was permitted to see his father, to whom he asked, "Why didn't she leave me alone?"

On August 28, Chambers was arraigned for the murder of Jennifer Levin. Many of his friends showed their support by attending the proceedings. Two weeks later a grand jury indicted Chambers on two separate counts of murder: murder with intent to kill, and murder "as the result of an act that showed a depraved indifference to human life."

"We believe that either one or both of these occurred," Manhattan District Attorney Robert Morgenthau said in an interview with *New York* magazine. Under the second count, the prosecution would not need to show that Chambers actually intended to kill Levin. In either case, Morgenthau said, the grand jury charged that Chambers asphyxiated Levin by applying a "substantial amount of pressure" to her neck "over a substantial amount of time."

If the grand jury had ample reason to indict Chambers, Chambers had ample support from friends and family who thought otherwise. No one, perhaps, believed in Chambers's innocence more than his mother, Phyllis. She went to work enlisting some divine help to get her son out of prison and back home, pending the trial.

Archbishop Ted McCarrick of Newark, New Jersey, and later the archbishop of Washington, stepped in. McCarrick had known the Chambers family since Phyllis's tenure as personal nurse to Terence Cardinal Cooke, and now he aided the family by writing a letter to support Robert's bail.

Interviews with Chambers's friends and supporters also characterized him not only as innocent of Levin's death, but also a victim. Had Robert taken Levin to the park to have sex with her? Not likely, friends argued. He'd had the entire house to himself on the fateful evening—why have sex in public, on the grass, near a museum? No, they had gone to the park to talk, friends and supporters explained. After all, he had left his jacket back at Dorrian's, had he not? Chambers's supporters also questioned whether the Levin–Chambers romance was as torrid as some said. Was it not merely casual? Robert had had a steady girlfriend until that night.

On October 1, Chambers was released on $150,000 bail, raised by family members and Dorrian's owner Jack Dorrian, under the recognizance of Monsignor Thomas Leonard, Chambers's teacher at St. David's. Soon after, local authorities disclosed that Chambers was under investigation in connection with at least ten East Side burglaries. Chambers had been questioned a year earlier but had not been arrested. Chambers's allies bristled at the timing of the announcement, arguing that Chambers would not receive a fair trial.

Levin's family and friends, conversely, argued that it was Jennifer Levin who did not receive "a fair trial." From the beginning of the case, the media and the defense team had looked warily at the late girl. New York tabloids fought for sales, boasting headlines that proclaimed the shocking murder "The Preppy Murder." *New York Daily News* headlines trumpeted Levin's purported lasciviousness with colorful headlines: "How Jennifer Courted Death" and "Sex Play Got Rough."

With a milieu of doubt surrounding Levin's chastity, defense attorney Jack Litman went to work. Litman, age forty-three, was a Harvard alum and former assistant D.A. He'd made headlines defending Richard Herrin, a Yale University student accused of murdering his former girlfriend, Bonnie Garland. Although Herrin had admitted to bludgeoning her to death, the jury showed a modicum of sympathy for him by convicting Herrin of manslaughter. Litman had tried to demonstrate that "Herrin's sense of identity was wrapped up in his relationship with the victim and that she had triggered his emotional collapse when she threatened to leave him." Litman's full-frontal attack on the victim became known as the "Blame the Victim" strategy.

In the Chambers–Levin case, Litman planned to show that the relationship between Chambers and Levin was merely casual, and Chambers had no motivation for killing her. Furthermore, Litman argued at Chambers's bail hearing that Levin had not been strangled by hand or with clothing such as a shirt. She was choked from behind, between Chambers's left bicep and forearm. Litman likened the maneuver to a rear-restraining choke hold used often by police. The effects of the hold can be deadly, however, if it is applied the wrong way and the restrained person resists. Levin, Litman said, was the type of person who resisted and fought back.

Litman's spin on the case disgusted many people. In 1985, New York City's rape laws were amended to restrict testimony pertinent to the victim's sexual history. The law did not, however, apply to murder cases. That left Litman's attack on Levin's integrity virtually unabated.

In November 1986, Litman learned that prosecutor Linda Fairstein had located Levin's personal diary. Rumors spread like a virus that this notebook contained graphic details of Levin's sexual encounters plus the names of many of her male partners. Litman said Fairstein had mentioned the book to him; Fairstein denied doing so. But the crafty defense lawyer knew he had a "smoking gun" in his hand, regardless of the book's actual content. To even mildly suggest Levin's sexual appetite, he knew, was nearly as good as proving Levin actually did enjoy rough sex. Litman requested to the court that the diary be made available to the defense, arguing that it was "beneficial to his client and therefore under the rules of evidence, he was entitled to it."

The press jumped all over this new development and dubbed the notebook "the Sex Diary." Fairstein rallied by telling reporters that the notebook was nothing more than a school date book that contained names and numbers of friends, and there was no book detailing her sex life. Eventually, the book in question was turned over to Justice Howard E. Bell for personal inspection. After reading the diary, Bell ruled that the defense would not have access to the book. In fact, the diary "contained no admissible evidence and nothing that was relevant and material to the defendant's case."

The modus operandi of the defense disgusted many in the Levin camp; a support group who called themselves "Justice for Jennifer" even demonstrated outside the courtroom, protesting the manner in which the defense was portraying Levin.

Meanwhile, free on bail, Robert Chambers continued to live life as he always had—partying, going to bars with friends, hanging out in public New York spots. And why not? If the media had portrayed Levin as all but a tramp, it practically had canonized Chambers as a "Kennedy" type with "tremendous potential."

Chambers had nearly two years to make his case as the victim in the crime, and Litman did his part to postpone the start of the trial, filing numerous motions in Judge Bell's courtroom. A year went by; the prosecution grew frustrated, and the public grew both weary and wary. For two years, New Yorkers wondered if Chambers ever would go to trial. Of note, Justice Bell did rule Chambers's videotaped confession about the murder admissible in court, but with a few minor deletions.

More damaging than the videotaped confession or the tape containing Chambers's psychotic pajama party with the headless doll were the testimonies from witnesses and associates, and Chambers's sullied reputation. By the time the trial opened on January 4, 1988, Justice Bell and Jack Litman had raised the ire of the media—Bell for his often controversial rulings and Litman for his public "Blame the Victim" tactics.

Despite Litman's efforts to twist the facts, scientific evidence and the statements rendered by Levin's friends and other witnesses spelled the difference in the trial. Fairstein quickly sought to establish the state of the crime scene and the condition of the body. She marched to the stand a variety of police officers and forensics specialists to show that, based on the evidence at the crime scene, Chambers had committed the murder. But the crime scene investigation and handling of evidence was anything but perfect, and Litman jumped at the chance to undermine the integrity of some of the evidence put forth by Fairstein.

A number of Levin's friends and witnesses on hand at Dorrian's on the night of Levin's death also testified. But more than anything, the testimony of specialists help cast doubt on Chambers's innocence: medical examiner Dr. Maria Alandy, who testified regarding the post mortem examination, said that "compression of the victim's neck had to be substantial in order to effect death." Her testimony belied Chambers's claim that he had momentarily grabbed Levin by the neck before flipping her over him. Fairstein also sought professional opinion on Levin's injuries from Dr. Werner Spitz, the chief medical examiner for the city of Detroit.

Ironically, Litman had initially contacted Spitz to testify for the defense. But from their first dialogue, Spitz made it clear that he did not like Litman or his manner of communicating. Spitz's acrimonious feelings toward Litman sharpened with Spitz on the stand and Litman hurling one question after another, seeking any answers helpful to the defense. The dialogue grew heated, with neither man backing down. Litman continued to focus on the length of time it took to strangle Levin, but Spitz refused to tell him what he wanted to hear:

Litman: I'm challenging you, Doctor, to tell us how the blouse was tightened into a rope around her neck! Can you or can't you tell us which part was against the side of her neck?

Spitz: I can't tell you.

Litman: The fact is that you can't do it, can you?

Spitz: If you want, I'll demonstrate to you right now, on yourself!

With just five witnesses set to testify, Litman began his defense of Robert Chambers Jr. on March 2. Key to his case was the testimony of Dr. Ronald Kornblum, chief medical examiner for Los Angeles. Litman did his utmost to coerce Kornblum to refute Dr. Spitz's analyses and testimony. But was it enough?

Barely one week later, the defense rested, and the case went to the jury. For nine days, newspapers reported every conceivable detail of the trial, and columnists offered their opinions on how the jury would vote. The tension was palpable throughout the state, between the families involved, and, especially, in the deliberations room. Determining whether Robert Chambers Jr. would go free or to jail was a grueling task for a jury clearly uncertain which way to vote. At one stage of the deliberations, the vote was 8-4 for acquittal; then, a second poll was 9-3 for a conviction on second-degree murder. The tension became almost unbearable for some jurors. Many asked to leave the room even for a moment to escape the crushing pressure. According to reports, one black juror accused other members of the jury of being prejudiced.

But none felt the heat more than Chambers and Jack Litman. Litman's worries transcended the present murder trial; Chambers was still under investigation for a string of burglaries committed in 1986. Litman knew his client could spend years in jail—if not the remainder of his life—if convicted of the felony charges and manslaughter.

This time, Chambers could not rely on a guardian angel or his mother to rescue him—only on the desperate bargaining of his lawyer. During the nine-day deliberations, Litman worked quickly to make the best of two bad situations. He contacted Fairstein about plea bargaining a deal; on the ninth day of deliberations that deal surfaced in a buzzing courtroom. Chambers would plead guilty to first-degree manslaughter and guilty to one count of burglary for the robberies he committed in 1986. Overlooked, at the time, were the possible ramifications of the plea: should Chambers be convicted of a third felony, he would face life in prison.

With the jury out of the courtroom, Chambers stood before Judge Bell and addressed the question on everyone's mind: "Is it true, Mr.

Chambers, that on August 26, 1986, you intended to cause serious physical injury to Jennifer Levin and thereby causing her death?"

After responding a few times with convoluted statements that did not fully answer the question, Chambers finally replied: "Yes, Your Honor." He did so while shaking his head.

Sentencing was set for April 15. Later that evening, the jury returned to the courtroom to hear the surprising news. Some members of the panel cried as they left the box. Quickly, the media swarmed over the courtroom, seeking comments from anyone with a vested interest in the case.

Ellen Levin was one of the first to speak on camera about the decision. "I don't think we could have withstood another trial," she said, refering to her fear of a hung jury. "We could not have sustained that strain and tension for another year and a half." And yet, the story continued to live a life of its own. In April, Chambers was sentenced to serve five to fifteen years for manslaughter, "with the sentence for burglary being served concurrently." The Levin family later filed a $25 million wrongful death suit against Robert Chambers Jr. and won a judgment against any of his future income.

That same April, *A Current Affair* aired the now infamous "doll tape" and the world got a real glimpse of the practically perfect preppy Chambers's other side. Members of the media viewed the videotape and then proceeded to hammer away at Chambers's character for months to come. In 1989, a made-for-TV movie called *The Preppie Murder* was produced, starring William Baldwin as Chambers and Lara Flynn Boyle as Levin. The film was made without cooperation from most of those involved.

Robert Chambers Jr., meanwhile, was incarcerated at Auburn State Prison where he served every day of his fifteen-year sentence. Like his life on the streets, his time behind bars was anything but "lawful." An Associated Press report said that between July 1988 and July 1997 alone, Chambers "was docked for 75 months of good time due to seven violations of prison rules." All told, Chambers spent five years of his initial fifteen-year sentence in solitary confinement for bad behavior, and for protection from other inmates.

The story of the "Preppy Murder" could have ended there. Again, however, Chambers was unable to keep his nose clean—literally and figuratively. Upon his 2003 release from prison, he returned to New York City and moved into a high-rise on East 57th Street. In 2005, he was charged with heroin possession and served one hundred days in jail. Life on the seventeenth floor was what it had been at Choate and BU and the other schools that Chambers had turned into his own party zone. Neighbors often called the police to complain about the motley crews of oddballs that showed up at the front door of the building at all hours and ambled up the stairs to Chambers's apartment.

Finally, on October 22, 2007, police arrived at Chambers's apartment door, with a no-knock search warrant in hand and a battering ram at the ready. They broke down the door and arrested two people: forty-one-year-old Robert Chambers Jr. and his thirty-nine-year-old girlfriend, Shawn Kovell. According to published reports, Chambers struggled with police, who found on the premises crack pipes and several bags of cocaine. The *New York Daily News* called the apartment a den of "heavy drug traffic in recent months . . . undercover cops bought a quarter-kilo of coke with a street value of $20,000." The *New York Post*, however, reported that "in all, they purchased nearly $10,000 worth of drugs during seven different sales." Regardless of the exact figure, police sentenced Chambers to nineteen years in prison on criminal possession of a controlled substance, first degree.

Kovell, ironically, earned another shot at the proverbial fifteen minutes of fame. Also charged with selling drugs, she was one of the pretty, underwear-clad girls pictured in the videotape featured on *A Current Affair*. Now, like Robert Chambers Jr., she was earning her comeuppance for her own antisocial behavior.

Perhaps now the final chapter of the Preppy Murder has been written.

Bibliography

Books

Brussel, James A. *Casebook of a Crime Psychiatrist*. New York: Dell, 1968.

Cook, Adrian. *The Armies of the Streets: The New York City Draft Riots of 1863*. Lexington, KY: University of Kentucky Press, 1974.

Davis, John H. *Mafia Dynasty: The Rise and Fall of the Gambino Crime Family*. New York: HarperCollins, 1994.

Jones, Jack. *Let Me Take You Down: Inside the Mind of Mark David Chapman, the Man Who Killed John Lennon*. New York: Villard Books, 1992.

Kane, Larry. *Lennon Revealed*. New York: Running Press, 2005.

Klausner, Lawrence D. *Son of Sam: Based on the Authorized Transcription of the Tapes, Official Documents, and Diary of David Berkowitz*. New York: McGraw-Hill, 1980.

Lennon, Cynthia. *John*. New York: Crown, 2005.

Mustain, Gene, and Jerry Capeci. *Murder Machine*. New York: Onyx, 1993.

O'Brien, Joseph F., and Andris Kurins. *Boss of Bosses: The FBI and Paul Castellano*. New York: Simon & Schuster, 1991.

Raab, Selwyn. *Five Families: The Rise, Decline, and Resurgence of America's Most Powerful Mafia Empires*. New York: Thomas Dunne Books, 2005.

Rosenthal, A. M. *Thirty-Eight Witnesses: The Kitty Genovese Case*. Berkeley, CA: University of California Press, 1964.

Terry, Maury. *The Ultimate Evil: An Investigation into America's Most Dangerous Satanic Cult*. New York: Doubleday, 1987.

Wolfe, Linda. *Wasted: The Preppy Murder*. New York: Simon and Schuster, 1989.

Web sites

Bardsley, Marilyn. "Son of Sam, David Berkowitz, famous serial killer—Letter 17." *The Crime Library.* http://www.crimelibrary.com/serial_killers/ notorious/berkowitz/letter_17.html.

http://chicagoist.com/2005/05/10/whats_in_a_mobster_nickname.php

http://www.cnn.com/2008/CRIME/08/12/chapman.no.parole/index.html

Hockenberry, John. "Did 'Son of Sam' really act alone?" http://www.msnbc .msn.com/id/5351509

http://www.knowledgerush.com/kr/encyclopedia/George_P._Metesky/http:// www.rarenewspapers.com/view/554344

http://www.lib.jjay.cuny.edu/crimeinny/

www.newsday.com

"The Official Home Page of David Berkowitz." Forgivenforlife.org

www.People.com

www.time.com

www.trutv.com

Other Publications

American Heritage magazine
On The Media from NPR
New York Times
New York Daily News
New York Post
Waterbury Republican
Associated Press
Bloomberg News
Time magazine